C O N T E M P O R A R Y ' S

Obtaining Information and Using Resources

Series Developer
Lori Strumpf
President, Center for Remediation Design

Author
Kristine M. Mains

Project Editor
Cathy Niemet

CONTEMPORARY
BOOKS
CHICAGO

Library of Congress Cataloging-in-Publication Data

Strumpf, Lori.
    Esssential skills for the workplace. Obtaining information & using resources / Lori Strumpf & Kristine Mains.
        p.   cm.
    ISBN 0-8092-3903-5 (paper)
    1. Office practice—Handbooks, manuals, etc.   2. Office management—Handbooks, manuals, etc.   3. Business information services—Handbooks, manuals, etc.   4. Physical distribution of goods—Handbooks, manuals, etc.   5. Secretaries—Vocational guidance—Handbooks, manuals, etc.   I. Mains, Kristine.   II. Title.
    HF5547.5.S817   1993   93-24806
                                                                            CIP

Published by Contemporary Books, Inc.
Two Prudential Plaza, Chicago, Illinois 60601-6790
Manufactured in the United States of America
International Standard Book Number: 0-8092-3903-5

10   9   8   7   6   5   4   3

Published simultaneously in Canada by
Fitzhenry & Whiteside
195 Allstate Parkway
Markham, Ontario L3R 4T8
Canada

Editorial Director Caren Van Slyke	*Production Editor* Jean Farley Brown
Editorial Solveig Robinson Eunice Hoshizaki Lisa Black Lynn McEwan Craig Bolt	*Cover Design* Georgene Sainati *Illustrator* Graziano, Krafft & Zale, Inc.
Editorial Assistant Maggie McCann	*Art & Production* Todd Petersen Jan Geist
Editorial Production Manager Norma Fioretti	*Typography* Point West Carol Stream, Illinois

Cover photo © Westlight
Photo manipulation by Kristin Nelson, Provizion

Essential Skills for the Workplace stems from a national demonstration project conducted by the Center for Remediation Design (CRD), a joint project of the U.S. Conference of Mayors, the National Association of Private Industry Councils, the Partnership for Training and Employment Careers, and the National Association of Counties. The CRD's primary goal is to help employers and training providers link basic skills training to the needs of the workplace.

The Project of the States, conducted by the CRD, the Center for Human Resources at Brandeis University, and select JTPA entities since 1987, focuses on the use of reading, writing, computation, problem solving, and communication skills in the workplace. Competencies singled out by this project's labor market studies as being essential to a successful workforce are the foundation for the lessons in this series.

CONTENTS

ACKNOWLEDGMENTS

Index on page 19 reprinted by permission of American Technical Publishers, Inc.

Recipes on pages 20–21 are from *The Low Cholesterol Cookbook*, by Mabel Cavaiani (Chicago: Contemporary Books, 1980). Reprinted by permission of author.

Employee handbook excerpts on pages 24–34 reprinted by permission of JobSource.

Product label on page 49 reprinted by permission of Bausch & Lomb.

Product labels on pages 50 and 52 reprinted by permission of Burroughs Wellcome Company.

Product labels on page 51 reprinted by permission of Alljack Company.

Product labels on page 53 reprinted by permission of SmithKline Beecham.

Advertisement on page 54 reprinted by permission of Wickes Lumber Company.

Product label on page 55 reprinted by permission of A. H. Robins Company.

Brochure on page 56 reprinted by permission of General Tire.

Product labels on page 58 reprinted by permission of Walgreen Company.

Purchase orders on pages 64–65, 68 and 161 reprinted by permission of Decker's.

Advertisement on page 60 reprinted by permission of Cambridge Camera Exchange, Inc.

Advertisement on page 61 reprinted by permission of Weed Wizard, Inc.

Mileage distance chart on page 72 reprinted by permission of Illinois Department of Transportation.

Bus schedules on pages 74 and 80 reprinted by permission of CARTA (Chattanooga Area Regional Transportation Authority).

Shuttle bus schedule on page 78 reprinted by permission of Maryland Aviation Administration.

Receiving forms and bills of lading on pages 81, 87, 88–89, and 92 reprinted by permission of The Worth Corporation.

Pro forms on pages 81 and 88 reprinted by permission of Carter Express, Inc.

Yellow pages excerpts on pages 82–85 reprinted by permission of Ameritech Publishing Company.

Postal rate charts on pages 90–91 and 114–115 reprinted courtesy of the U.S. Postal Service.

Paychecks on pages 136–137 reprinted by permission of JobSource.

TO THE LEARNER

Contemporary's *Essential Skills for the Workplace* series has four books—two books in Level One, two books in Level Two. Each book **integrates,** or combines, the reading, math, writing, communication, and problem-solving skills you need to complete tasks at the workplace and in everyday life.

Essential Skills for the Workplace will take you out of the classroom and into the world of work. Each task in these books is a task you may encounter at the workplace. In addition, each task is part of the "big picture"—part of the process required to make a business purchase, for example, or to prepare a business delivery.

This book, *Obtaining Information and Using Resources*, is part of Level One of the series. In this book, you'll work with charts, schedules, documents, and measuring devices used in many jobs and in everyday life. You'll practice the skills you need to complete basic tasks in the workplace. When you finish the two workbooks in Level One, you'll be ready for Level Two. At this level, you will actually focus on a specific type of job. You will use the basic skills learned in Level One to help you complete several projects involved with a certain type of job.

In Level One, you will

- be guided through basic workplace tasks
- practice the skills needed to complete these tasks
- apply these skills to a related task

Features in Level One include

- a Skill Preview that tells you what each lesson is about
- a Skill Mastery that lets you demonstrate your skills
- Self-Check suggestions that help you check your work
- Workwise activities that help you think about the world of work
- a Glossary that defines more than 100 workplace-related terms

In the back of the book, you'll find an answer key and blank copies of some important forms and documents.

We hope you enjoy *Essential Skills for the Workplace Level One: Obtaining Information and Using Resources*. We wish you the best of luck with your studies.

The Editors

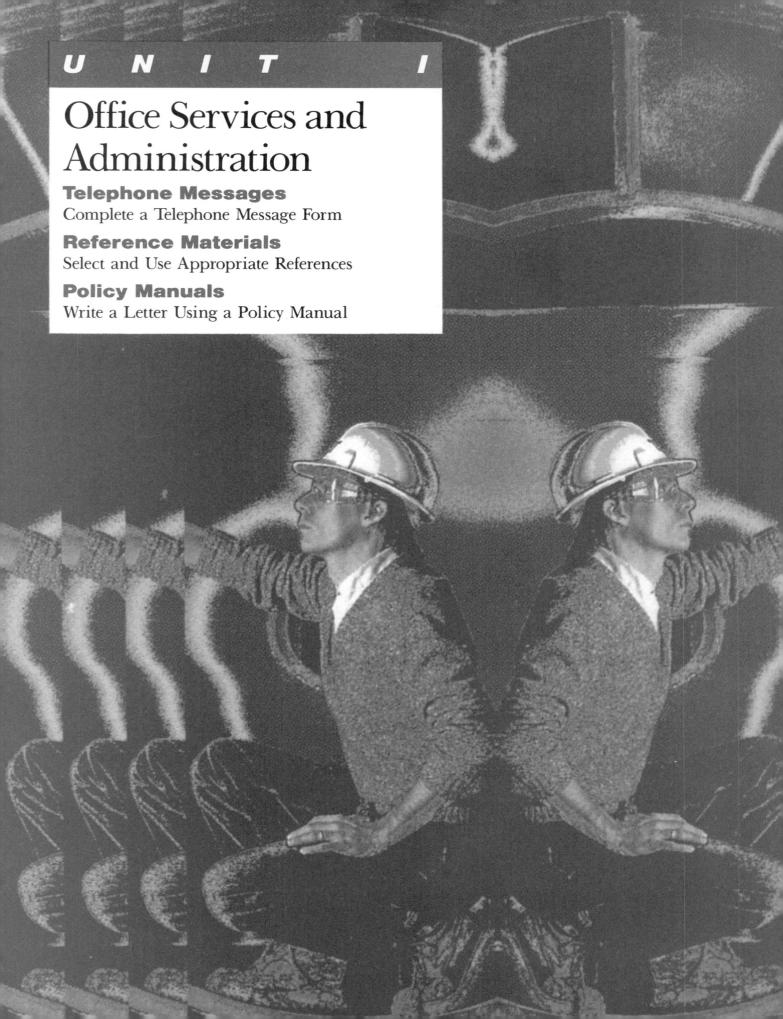

UNIT I

Office Services and Administration

Telephone Messages
Complete a Telephone Message Form

Reference Materials
Select and Use Appropriate References

Policy Manuals
Write a Letter Using a Policy Manual

TELEPHONE MESSAGES

Have you ever had a hard time trying to take a telephone message? Maybe there was too much noise in the background, or the caller did not speak clearly.

Telephone messages are often about important meetings, clients, arrangements, or supplies. Taking an incorrect message can cost your company time and money.

SKILL PREVIEW

What information does a telephone message include? How is the information recorded? How is the message sent?

Read the scene and dialogue. Then answer the questions.

Scene
It is April 3 at 2:45 P.M. at the Ace Printing Company. The receptionist answers the phone.

Dialogue
"Ace Printing. May I help you?"

"I want to speak to John Williams."

"He isn't in. May I take a message?"

"Yes. Tell him that George Lee called. I need an extra 1,000 envelopes on this month's order. He can call me at (612) 555-5609."

"Yes, sir. You need a thousand envelopes and you can be reached at (612) 555-5609?"

"That's right."

"Thank you. I'll give him the message."

1. Who is calling?

   _____

2. Who is the call for?

   _____

3. What is the message?

   _____

   _____

4. When was the call made?

   _____

   _____

5. What is the person's telephone number?

   _____

RECEIVING SPOKEN INSTRUCTIONS

Telephone **messages** involve at least two people: the sender and the receiver. A person who calls in with a message is the sender. When you answer a telephone call, you take a message for the receiver. The sender often gives you a set of **instructions** to write down for the receiver.

How can you be sure you are hearing and writing the correct instructions?

- *Repeat* the instructions.
- *Clarify* the instructions with questions.
- *Write* the instructions on a message form.

GUIDED PRACTICE

Suppose your boss's wife calls her husband. He is in a meeting, so you take a message for him.

Mrs. Greene says: "Ask my husband to let me know if he is leaving work today at 5:00 P.M. If he is, I'd like him to pick me up at home before we go out to dinner. Otherwise, I'll meet him there. He can call me back this morning at my office."

What message or instructions would you give to your boss? Write the information in your own words:

_____

_____

_____

You are correct if you wrote something like: *Mr. Greene, your wife wants you to call her this morning at work about tonight's dinner plans.*

What questions could you ask to clarify the message or instructions?

1. _____

_____

2. _____

_____

You're correct if you wrote something like: *"Does your husband have your number at work? If your husband can't call you back until this afternoon, where can he reach you?"*

When you take telephone messages, you do not need to repeat every word you hear from the sender. Listen for the **key points**.

Read the message. Then write the key points of the message on the lines below.

Telephone Message

"Please check with the plant manager, the shift chief, and the quality control inspector. See if they are free for a meeting in my office at 10:00 tomorrow morning. Otherwise, set up the meeting for 10:00 on Wednesday morning."

Instructions: _____

_____

_____

Suggested times: _____ or _____

Who is involved: 1. _____ 2. _____

3. _____

APPLIED PRACTICE 2: CLARIFYING THE MESSAGE

By asking questions, you can make sure that you have heard the key points of the message correctly. By repeating or restating the key points, you are **clarifying**, or making the message clear.

Suppose Mr. Canty is the plant manager, Mr. Smith is the shift chief, and Ms. James is the quality control inspector. How could you restate the message as a question?

_____

_____

_____

. . . .
Oral Communication: Receiving spoken instructions in the workplace
Writing: Recording essential information in phrases or simple sentence form accurately and precisely

RECORDING ESSENTIAL INFORMATION

The most **essential**, or important, information in a telephone message is the name of the caller and the correct telephone number. Be sure that the intended receiver gets this information written correctly.

GUIDED PRACTICE

When you call telephone numbers in your local region, you do not have to dial an **area code** first. But when you call numbers outside your region, you do have to dial 1 plus a three-digit area code before you dial the other numbers. Area codes are written in three ways, either set off by parentheses ( ), by a slash /, or by a hyphen -: (308)969-3321, 308/969-3321, or 308-969-3321.

Circle the area code in the phone numbers below.

312/695-3213   239-2147   613-779-2617

(212)332-4931   642/908-7521   549-0762

You are correct if you circled the area codes: *312, 613, 212,* and *642.*

APPLIED PRACTICE 3: RECORDING NUMBERS CAREFULLY

Write the following telephone numbers carefully.

1. Area code: six, three, nine Number: eight, eight, two, four, one, zero, two

   (   )_____

2. Area code: two, zero, two Number: six, three, six, zero, two, zero, three

   (   )_____

3. Area code: five, three, zero Number: seven, nine, six, two, four, zero, eight

   (   )_____

Telephone messages often include the six basic questions news writers use: *who? what? when? where? why?* and *how?*

Read the telephone message. Write the words *how, when, why, what,* and *where* on the lines next to the information that answers each question. The *who* questions are done for you.

To __Len Hayes__

Date __5/20__   Time __9:00 A.M.__

WHILE YOU WERE OUT

M __Stan Dawkins__

of __Penn Printing Co.__

Phone __(416)   298-3547__

Area Code   Number   Extension

TELEPHONED		✓	PLEASE CALL	
CALLED TO SEE YOU			WILL CALL AGAIN	
WANTS TO SEE YOU			URGENT	
	RETURNED YOUR CALL			

Message __He will deliver booklets you need for tomorrow's meeting by messenger service today.__

__Fannie Gray__
Operator

who? __Len Hayes__

_____

who? __Stan Dawkins__

_____

_____

_____

You were correct if you wrote: *when* next to the "Date" and "Time" line; *what* next to the check-off section; and *why* and *how* next to the message part of the form.

SELF-CHECK

To ensure accuracy, repeat the number for the caller *after* you write it down. Fewer errors occur than if you repeat the number while you are writing it down.

News items often have to be reduced to fit a specific space in the newspaper. And yet the news items must still include the most essential facts from the original article. Well-written news items answer the six basic questions: *who? what? where? when? why?* and *how?*

Read the message. Then fill in only the essential information.

Mr. Jones: "Mr. Trask, your attorney, called to tell you that you and your partner must sign the two contracts you requested by the close of business tomorrow in your attorney's office. Send them by messenger to meet the deadline ."

Essential Information:

Who called: _____

What: _____

Where: _____

When: _____

Why: _____

How: _____

When a specific time is part of the message, write hour:minutes, followed by A.M. for morning (midnight to noon) or P.M. (noon to midnight). For example, eight o'clock in the morning (8:00 A.M.); one-forty in the afternoon (1:40 P.M.).

Phrases about time used in the workplace include: "by close of business," "before noon," and "during office hours." You can clarify what these phrases mean by asking, "What are your office hours?" Then record: "Between 8:00 A.M. and 5:00 P.M."

Write the time accurately on the lines below.

1. Four-thirty in the afternoon ____:____ ____.____.

2. A quarter to ten in the morning ____:____ ____.____.

3. Eleven o'clock tonight ____:____ ____.____.

4. Eight forty-five tomorrow morning ____:____ ____.____.

. . . .

Writing: Entering appropriate information onto a form; Transferring numbers onto appropriate sections of forms

COMPLETING A TELEPHONE MESSAGE FORM

Most workplaces use a standard form to record messages. The names of the caller and the receiver, the person's telephone number, and his or her company are included.

GUIDED PRACTICE

Write the words *caller, telephone number, receiver,* and *company name* on the blank lines next to where the information is shown.

To Jan Jacobs

Date_____ Time_____

WHILE YOU WERE OUT

Mr. Samuels

of Zenith One Products

Phone (312) 668-4935

Area Code   Number   Extension

You were correct if you wrote: *receiver,* first; *caller,* second; *company name,* third; and *telephone number,* on the last line.

APPLIED PRACTICE 6: WRITING LEGIBLY

Look at the sample form below and answer the questions.

WHILE YOU WERE OUT

M_____

of_____

Phone _____

Area Code   Number   Extension

TELEPHONED	PLEASE CALL	✓
CALLED TO SEE YOU	WILL CALL AGAIN	✓
WANTS TO SEE YOU	URGENT	
	RETURNED YOUR CALL	

Message_____

Who called?

_____

What is the telephone number?

_____

What is the message?

_____

To make a message complete, check for errors and make sure all the information has been filled in.

Read the message on the form below. There are four elements missing. Ask a series of questions about the missing elements.

TO: _____Anne_____

Time: _____7:45_____   Date: _____2/4/93_____

Please Call:

_____Angela_____

Telephone # _____751-2708_____

Message: _Meet me at youth center_
Need tutors for community service contract.

1. _____
2. _____
3. _____
4. _____

WORKWISE

Select a local business and ask if you can interview a receptionist about his or her telephone message-taking procedure. Compare your procedure for taking and delivering messages with those of the person you interview. Write a summary of your comparison.

SETTING UP A SYSTEM FOR MESSAGES

If a system for how messages are to be transmitted does not exist at your company, it would be good for you to take initiative and implement one.

GUIDED PRACTICE

Read the following situation and decide which action you would take. Circle the letter of the best choice.

Ralph, a receptionist in a large real estate office, takes complete, legible messages. However, he keeps them stacked on his desk and delivers them only twice a day (before noon and before closing). Several clients have been lost due to delays in salespersons getting back to them. The sales staff blames Ralph; Ralph blames them. What should Ralph do?

    a. Since Ralph takes messages for everyone, he should insist that the sales staff pick up their messages at his desk.

    b. Ralph should take the messages to the sales staff once every hour.

You are correct if you said: *choice **b** would please the sales staff more. It would also ensure that the sales staff received their messages more frequently.*

APPLIED PRACTICE 8: SUGGESTING A SOLUTION

Read the situation. Suggest a solution to the problem.

Kim, an editor at a publishing company, works on one floor and the receptionist works on another floor. Kim must answer her calls by the fourth ring or her calls go back to the receptionist. Kim often misses her calls because she works at a computer away from her desk. Kim often does not get her messages until late in the day or sometimes not until the next day. This system does not work well for Kim or her company.

Suggested solution: _____

_____

_____

....
Reading: Making inferences from text

COMPLETE A TELEPHONE MESSAGE FORM

Complete the telephone message form below, using the information given in the scene and the dialogue.

Scene
It is ten minutes to eleven on the morning of February second. Kim Wong is calling Ray Douglas, who is not in the office. Kim is president of First Central Bank.

Dialogue
"Good morning. This is Lynn Moon. May I help you?"

"Yes. This is Kim Wong. Tell Ray we are ready to go on his loan, but I need a go-ahead from him with at least an hour's notice."

"OK. I'll have him call you back when he returns to the office. At what number can Mr. Douglas reach you?"

"I'm at (454)232-0800."

"You're at (454)232-0800?"

"That's right."

"I'll tell Mr. Douglas to call you about his loan."

```
TO: _____

Time: _____  Date: _____

Please Call:

_____

Telephone # _____

Message: _____

_____

_____


                        Operator:
```

REFERENCE MATERIALS

Often on a job you need more information before you can do a task. You need to refer to other books, guides, manuals, files, or computer printouts called **reference materials**.

Knowing how to select and use the right references when you are looking for information will improve your job performance. It will also save your company time and money.

SKILL PREVIEW

How do you get the information you need from reference materials? What process will help you locate the information you are looking for quickly and efficiently? Show what you already know about reference materials.

Circle the word that matches each description.

1. A general list of topics at the front of a book
   title   table of contents

2. To read quickly to find specific information
   scan   caption

3. The name of a book, manual, or reference source
   title   index

4. An alphabetical list of topics at the back of a book
   index   scan

5. The explanation or description of a photo or diagram
   caption   skim

6. To read quickly through a text to find out what it's about, in general
   skim   index

7. A box of text containing information about a topic
   chart   table of contents

SELECTING APPROPRIATE REFERENCES

Reading the **title**, or name, of a book or manual can help you decide if you have found the reference that might have the information you need.

GUIDED PRACTICE

If you needed to find a reference book for the three tasks listed below, which title would you choose for each?

- *Computer Manual*
- *Zip Code Directory*
- *Webster's Dictionary*
- *Nursing Assistant Manual*

- *Workplace Safety Handbook*
- *Copier Operations Manual*
- *Machine Repair Manual*
- *Employee's Insurance and Dental Benefits Handbook*

1. Finding the correct spelling of a word for a report _____

2. Understanding your company's dental insurance plan _____

3. Using an instruction book about an office copying machine _____

You are correct if you chose: 1. *Webster's Dictionary*; 2. *Employee's Insurance and Dental Benefits Handbook*; and 3. *Copier Operations Manual*.

APPLIED PRACTICE 1: SELECTING REFERENCE MATERIALS

From the reference titles listed above, choose the book title you would refer to for performing each task.

1. performing the duties of a nurse's aide _____

2. repairing a broken motor _____

3. finding a regional area number _____

4. filling out an accident report form _____

5. formatting a disk _____

USING A TABLE OF CONTENTS

A **table of contents** appears at the front of a reference book. It lists the general topics included in the book.

CONTENTS

Shown on page 17 is a table of contents with two columns. Skim each line in the first column across and go down to the next line. Do the same with column two. In each line, read the chapter number, then the topic, and then the page number where the topic begins.

Skim the table of contents on page 17 to find the correct answers.

1. Which *chapter* deals with making a menu?   22   28

2. Which *page* begins the reference to appetizers?   84   529

You are correct if you circled: 1. *28*; and 2. *84.*

APPLIED PRACTICE 2: READING A TABLE OF CONTENTS

Skim the table of contents on page 17 to find the correct answers.

_____ 1. In which chapters are four meat preparations discussed?

_____ 2. To read about personal cleanliness, which chapter should you consult?

_____ 3. On what page is the index?

_____ 4. Which chapter tells how to make pie doughs and fillings?

_____ 5. To learn about herbs and spices, on which page should you look?

_____ 6. Which chapter covers the preparation of fish and shellfish?

_____ 7. Which page begins the reference to equipment needed?

_____ 8. If you want to learn how to make sauces and gravies, which chapter should you consult?

_____ 9. Which three chapters discuss pies, cakes, and puddings?

....

SELF-CHECK

Did you remember that the chapter number appears first, then the topic, and finally, the page number where the topic begins? Did you look for the topic first and then the page number?

....

. . . .

Reading: Using table of contents, index, appendices, glossary, systems or subsystems

USING AN INDEX

Using an index is a quick way to see if a book contains the information you need. An **index** appears at the back of a reference book. It lists topics in alphabetical order and gives the page numbers where each topic can be found.

GUIDED PRACTICE

You work for a catering service and have been asked to plan a holiday party. You might look at an index like the one shown below to see if it has information you can use to complete your task. What pages deal with menu planning?

Meat salad, julienne 147	Mushroom soup, cream of 204–205	Oriental sweet-sour sauce 319–320
Meat salads 146–150		Osso bucco 383–384
Meat saw 16	Mushroom sauce 287; with beef tenderloin 351–352	Ounces, fractional, rounding off 66
Meat tenderizer, hand 20	Mushrooms, stuffed 94	Oven brown potatoes 266
Meat turner 17	Mustard sauce 290	Oxtail 334; soup 211–212; stew 348–349
Melba sauce 319	Mustard seed 118	
Melon-ball cocktail 91–92	Mutton stock 192	Oyster bisque 214
Melon ball scoop 18		Oysters casino, baked 99
Melon-grape cocktail 92	**N**	Oyster cocktail 92
Menu planning 646–649	Napolitaine sauce 304	Oyster knife 16
Menu types 645–646	Navarin of lamb 436–437	Oyster stuffing 476
Menu writing 649–652; suggestions for 651–652	Neufchâtel cheese 172	Oysters 484–485, 497; grades 485; fried 510; purchasing 484–486; shucking 484–485
Meringue toppings 592–593	New England clam chowder 221–222	
Meuniere sauce 310–311	Newburg sauce 290–291	Oysters Rockefeller 98
Microwave oven 31	New York butter cream icing 614	Oysters, scalloped 515
Milanaise sauce 304–305		
Milk, for pie dough 568; how		

index 673

You are correct if you answered: *pages 646-649.*

1. What page shows how to make stuffed mushrooms? ____

2. What page shows how to make oven brown potatoes? ____

You are correct if you answered: 1. *94*; and 2. *266.*

APPLIED PRACTICE 3: READING AN INDEX

Use the same index to find the page numbers for these parts of a party meal.

1. meringue pie toppings ____

2. New England clam chowder ____

3. oysters Rockefeller ____

4. melon-grape cocktail ____

5. meat salads ____

6. beef tenderloin with mushroom sauce ____

. . . .
Reading: Identifying factual details and specifications within text

SKIMMING FOR INFORMATION

You can **skim**, or read quickly, through a text to find out what it is about, in general. Also look at heads and subheads, and at type that is in **bold** type or in *italics*.

GUIDED PRACTICE

As you read this cookbook excerpt, skim the heading and the text. Then circle the choice that best tells what it is about.

Broiling Ham Slices

With a sharp knife, remove all visible fat from a center cut of ham, which has been cut about 1-inch thick. Broil the ham about 2 inches from heat, turning once while broiling. For fully cooked ham, broil 15 minutes. For uncooked ham, broil 25 minutes.

---

1. How to trim fat from ham slices   2. How to broil ham slices

You were correct if you circled choice 2, *how to broil ham slices.*

APPLIED PRACTICE 4: SKIMMING

Skim the following text. Then circle the number of the choice that tells what each paragraph is about.

Preparing Fish

Fish should be cooked at a low or moderate heat. If it is cooked at too high a temperature or for too long it will get dry and tough.

It is easy to tell when fish is cooked. Raw fish has a watery, translucent look. After it has been cooked, fish becomes opaque and milky white, and the flesh separates easily into layers or flakes. If there are any bones in the fish, the flesh will fall away from the bones easily. Most cooked fish tends to break easily so it should be handled with care.

Paragraph 1:

1. Why you should cook fish at a high temperature

2. Why you should cook fish at a low temperature

Paragraph 2:

1. Why fish breaks easily   2. How to tell when fish is cooked

SCANNING FOR INFORMATION

When you **scan** for information, you read quickly to find *specific* information. Look at numbers and amounts, ingredients, and cooking time.

GUIDED PRACTICE

Scan the following recipe and answer the questions that follow.

Roast Chicken

1	4-pound roasting chicken	1	small onion
½	teaspoon salt	½	teaspoon ground thyme
⅛	teaspoon pepper	¼	cup (½ stick) melted margarine

Wash the chicken, drain it, and remove all the fat with a sharp knife, but do not remove the skin. Sprinkle the inside of the chicken with salt and pepper. Put the onion inside the chicken and then truss the chicken. Place the chicken on a rack in a roasting pan in the oven. Bake the chicken in a preheated, moderate oven (350°F) for about 1¼ hours to 1½ hours or until the legs of the chicken will move easily. Combine the thyme with the melted margarine and use it to baste the chicken about every 15 minutes while it is baking. *Serves 6.*

_____ 1. How many pounds of chicken do you need for this recipe?

_____ 2. How many people does this recipe serve?

You are correct if you answered: 1. *4*; and 2. *6.*

APPLIED PRACTICE 5: SCANNING

Scan the recipe above to answer the questions.

1. At what temperature should the chicken be roasted? _____

2. How long should the chicken cook? _____

3. About how often should the chicken be basted? _____

4. Which vegetable is used in the recipe? _____

. . . .
Reading: Skimming or scanning to determine whether or not text contains relevant information

READING CHARTS

Knowing how to locate information on a chart or a computer printout is an important skill in most workplaces.

You read each row across from left to right. You read each column down from top to bottom. Each row and each column has a **heading**, or title.

A row across (**Striped Bass**) and a column down (**Calories**) have been shaded to show how to read them.

FISH AND SEAFOOD

Species	Calories	Protein (Grams)	Fat (Grams)	Cholesterol (Milligrams)
Snails	75	14.40	1.90	N/A
Snapper	100	20.51	1.34	37
Sole	91	18.84	1.19	48
Squid	92	15.58	1.38	233
Striped Bass	97	17.73	2.33	80
Swordfish	121	19.80	4.01	39
Trout (Rainbow)	118	20.55	3.36	57
Tuna (Bluefin)	144	23.33	4.90	38
Tuna (Skipjack)	103	22.00	1.01	47
Tuna (Yellowfin)	108	23.38	0.95	45

GUIDED PRACTICE

Use the chart to answer the following questions.

1. How many species of fish and seafood are shown on the chart? _____

2. What five categories are headings across the top of the chart?

   a. _____   b. _____   c. _____

   d. _____   e. _____

3. How many calories, grams of protein, grams of fat, and milligrams of cholesterol are in bluefin tuna?

a. _____ calories   c. _____ grams of fat

b. _____ grams of protein   d. _____ milligrams of cholesterol

You are correct if you answered: 1. *8*; 2. a. *species*, b. *calories*, c. *protein grams*, d. *fat grams*, and e. *cholesterol milligrams*; and 3. a. *144*, b. *23.33*, c. *4.90*, and d. *38*.

APPLIED PRACTICE 6: SCANNING A CHART

Use the chart on page 22 to answer the questions.

_____ 1. How many grams of protein are in snails?

_____ 2. Does snapper or swordfish contain more protein?

_____ 3. How many milligrams of cholesterol are in striped bass?

_____ 4. Does bluefin tuna or squid have less cholesterol?

_____ 5. How many fat grams are in rainbow trout?

_____ 6. Which fish has less fat, sole or bluefin tuna?

_____ 7. How many calories are in sole?

_____ 8. Does sole or rainbow trout have fewer calories?

_____ 9. Which fish has more cholesterol, snapper or squid?

_____ 10. Which fish has more protein, snails or swordfish?

_____ 11. Which fish has less fat, bluefin tuna or striped bass?

_____ 12. How many calories does rainbow trout have?

....

SELF-CHECK

To find the names of various fish, did you look down the row titled *species*? To find the numbers in each category, did you look down the row of the category being asked about?

....

. . . .

Reading: Locating pages, titles, paragraphs, figures, or charts to answer questions or solve problems

SELECT AND USE APPROPRIATE REFERENCES

Use the Employee Handbook Table of Contents to answer the following questions.

_____ 1. How many sections are there in the handbook?

_____ 2. Which page covers how much time you get off if a family member dies?

_____ 3. Which section discusses jury duty?

_____ 4. Which page covers employee savings plans?

_____ 5. Which section discusses company insurance plans?

WORKWISE

Select a reference at your workplace—for example, a computer manual. Skim the table of contents, index, charts, or illustrations. Choose one topic (function) you would like to learn more about and scan for specific information.

POLICY MANUALS

Have you ever been in a situation where you weren't sure what was expected of you? It could have been because you weren't given enough information. Maybe you weren't sure what someone said.

Because there are different kinds of people who work for the same company, certain basic policies and procedures are established to

- make job responsibilities and expectations clear,
- promote "time-saving" methods among employees, and
- provide structure for employee **performance evaluations**.

An **employee handbook** or **policy manual** includes company policies and procedures. When you become an employee of a company, you should read and ask questions about policies.

SKILL PREVIEW

You've planned a vacation leave from your job from July 24 to 30. Read the information from the policy manual below. Then fill out the request form. Your supervisor is Donna Novak, manager of the sporting goods department.

> **Vacation Leave:** A request for vacation shall be submitted to the employee's immediate supervisor no later than two weeks prior to the intended vacation leave. Vacation leave may be taken only after approval by the respective department head. The employee shall submit desired number of days and dates of vacation leave on the appropriate form designated by the Department of Human Resources. No other form of request will be accepted.

```
VACATION REQUEST FORM

Employee's name:_____  Date submitted: _____
Vacation dates/time requested: _____
Employee's signature: _____
Department:_____  Supervisor's name: _____
-------------------------------------------------------------------
Supervisor's signature: _____
Approved:  Yes / No    Date dis/approved: _____
```

UNDERSTANDING THE PURPOSE OF POLICY

A **policy** is a rule, plan, or course of action. Why should a company provide policy information for its employees?

The purpose of a policy manual is to explain

- what the company or organization stands for
- what the company expects from the employee
- how the employee's performance will be measured

Every aspect of employment is in a policy manual. Examples are

- application and hiring procedures
- conditions of employment (for example, working hours, sick leave, or vacation time)
- pay plans, salaries, and benefits
- employee performance evaluations and conduct

GUIDED PRACTICE

Using the information above, fill in the blanks.

Example: A policy is a ___rule___ , ___plan___ , or ___course of action___ .

1. The purpose of a policy manual is to explain
   a. what the company or organization _____
   b. what the company _____
   c. how the employee's _____

2. A policy manual contains
   a. application and _____
   b. conditions of _____
   c. pay plans, _____ , and _____
   d. employee_____ and _____

You are correct if you answered: 1. a. *stands for*, b. *expects from the employee*, c. *performance will be measured.* 2. a. *hiring procedures*, b. *employment*, c. *salaries, benefits*, d. *performance evaluations, conduct.*

WORKWISE

Look at the policy manual from your workplace or one from a friend. Make notes about its pay schedule, vacation leave, and medical/dental plans.

Use the information on the previous page to answer these questions.

1. In your own words, what is a policy? _____

   _____

2. Give one reason why employee handbooks or policy manuals are needed.

   _____

   _____

Use the policy manual page below to answer the questions.

Section <u>A</u> - <u>Purpose</u>

The purpose of this Personnel Policy Manual is to establish a high degree of understanding, cooperation, efficiency, service and unity that comes through the systematic application of workable guidelines for the control of personnel activities for JobSource. The fundamental objectives of personnel administration and these rules are:

1. to promote an esprit de corps that comes with discipline;

2. to promote and increase economy and efficiency in JobSource services;

3. to provide fair and equal opportunity to all qualified people;

4. to develop a program of recruitment, advancement, and tenure that will make JobSource's service attractive as a career, and encourage each employee to give her/his best service to JobSource to the ultimate betterment of the County of Madison; and

5. to advise the Commissioners and Directors, on all personnel affairs and policies.

---

1. Why does the policy manual state a set of workable guidelines?

   _____

2. Which objective shows that the company is open to all kinds of people?

   _____

   _____

. . . .
Reading: Identifying factual details and specifications within text

READING A POLICY MANUAL'S TABLE OF CONTENTS AND INDEX

Most policy manuals include these items:

- table of contents and/or index for easy reference
- pay plan (wage per hour, salary information, raises)
- benefits/compensation information (insurance, bonuses)
- description of an employee performance evaluation process
- expectations about employee conduct and disciplinary actions
- conditions of employment (work hours, sick leave, resignation)
- organization structure (who reports to whom, seniority)

GUIDED PRACTICE

A table of contents tells what topics are covered. Skim through the table of contents. Then write the chapter number for each piece of information listed below. (The roman numerals I to XIII represent the numbers 1 to 13.)

```
                        TABLE OF CONTENTS

    CHAPTER      I      GENERAL PROVISIONS

    CHAPTER      II     DEFINITION OF TERMS

    CHAPTER      III    POSITION CLASSIFICATION PLAN

    CHAPTER      IV     PAY PLAN

    CHAPTER      V      APPLICATIONS

    CHAPTER      VI     PROBATIONARY PERIOD

    CHAPTER      VII    EMPLOYEE PERFORMANCE EVALUATION

    CHAPTER      VIII   SEPARATION AND REINSTATEMENT

    CHAPTER      IX     DISCIPLINARY ACTION

    CHAPTER      X      EMPLOYEE DEVELOPMENT AND WELFARE ACTIVITIES

    CHAPTER      XI     CONDITIONS OF EMPLOYMENT

    CHAPTER      XII    VEHICLE ASSIGNMENT AND TRAVEL POLICIES

    CHAPTER      XIII   CONDUCT OF EMPLOYEES
```

Example: ___III (3)___ how positions are classified

1. _____ conditions of employment

2. _____ employee performance review information

3. _____ what happens if you are rude to customers

4. _____ employee conduct expectations

You were correct if you wrote: 1. *XI (11)*; 2. *VII (7)*; 3. *IX (9)*; 4. *XIII (13)*.

Most policy manuals have an index at the back of the book. The index tells you on which page to find various items of information. Skim the index to complete the statements below.

1. Hours of work are found in Chapter _____ on page _____.

2. Chapter _____ , section _____ , covers promotions.

3. Overtime information is found on pages _____ and _____.

4. Chapter _____ , section _____ , covers retirement fund information.

5. Pay period information is found in Chapter IV, section _____.

6. Chapter _____ , section _____ , covers information about employees who do excellent work or have been on the job for a long time.

. . . .
Reading: Using table of contents, index, appendices, glossary, systems, or subsystems

UNDERSTANDING A POLICY MANUAL

Policy manuals often include confusing terms or words. A **glossary** is usually included in the manual to help you identify and understand key words.

Policy manuals are divided into **chapters** and sometimes even further into shorter **sections** that cover one or two related topics. To understand the main idea of a paragraph or section, you should follow these steps:

1. *Skim* the whole section first.
2. *Make note* of any headings or titles with key words or phrases.
3. *Mark* or *highlight* any unfamiliar words or terms.
4. *Find the definition,* or meaning, of unfamiliar terms.
5. *Reread* the section until you feel you understand it.

GUIDED PRACTICE

Practice the five steps above as you read this manual entry. First, skim through the whole section. Then, answer the questions that follow.

┌ Heading: topic of the reading

```
Section C - Reasons for Disciplinary Action

If an employee's conduct falls below a desirable standard, they may be
subject to disciplinary action.  Any action reflecting discredit on
JobSource, or is a hindrance to the county governmental function such
as misconduct, inefficiency, incompetence, insubordination, indolence,
malfeasance, or willful violation of these rules, may be cause for
disciplinary action.  Some general things for which an employee may be
disciplined and/or dismissed are:
```

1. What is the heading of this section? _____

2. List any words that are unfamiliar to you.

    _____

3. Use the glossary to find the definition of at least one unfamiliar word. Write the definition here.

    _____

4. Reread the section. Do you feel you understand it? If not, discuss the section with a classmate or with your instructor.

You are correct if you wrote: 1. *Reasons for Disciplinary Action;* 2–4. Answers will vary.

Skim the following section of a policy manual. Make a check mark (✔) by any headings or titles. Circle any unfamiliar terms. Then answer the questions.

Section D - Disciplinary Steps

Discipline must be administered uniformly and indiscriminately. Efforts should be concentrated on preventing problems from occurring rather than disciplining employees for misconduct or poor performance. However, when discipline does become necessary, disciplinary action will be applied progressively except when the violation is serious enough to warrant immediate action. The steps of progression are as follows:

1.   Oral Warning - In a private session between supervisor and employee, problem areas shall be outlined for the employee, including expected behavior, and standards and goals that are not being met. Within five working days, the employee shall be sent a letter summarizing the conversation.

2.   Written Warning - Upon the second occurrence (within one year) or continued deficiency, in a private session, the supervisor will issue to the employee a written reprimand outlining problem areas and expected behavior. The employee will be requested to sign the letter acknowledging its receipt only. A copy will be placed in the employees Personnel File.

---

1. What is the main purpose of this section? _____

   _____

2. The first sentence states that discipline must be given *uniformly* and *indiscriminately*. If you need to, look up the definitions of these two words in the dictionary. Then rewrite the sentence in your own words.

   _____

   _____

3. Who is involved in an oral warning? _____

   _____

4. What happens to a written reprimand once the employee has signed it? Why do you think this is so?

   _____

   _____

. . . .

Reading: Following sequential directions to complete a task; Determining the main idea of a paragraph or section

IDENTIFYING SEQUENTIAL DIRECTIONS

In a manual, directions may be listed in an easy-to-read **outline**. Or procedures may be written in paragraphs. When you need to follow a paragraph of directions:

- *Read* carefully.
- Try *rewriting* the directions or procedures in a list (look for commas, semicolons, periods, or the word *and* to set apart a step).
- *Reread* the paragraph and list to check that the steps are in the correct order.

GUIDED PRACTICE

Read the following procedures for a work program.

Procedures for Work Program
Counselor will identify clients appropriate for program and make a referral to the Program Director. The Program Director will place the client in the appropriate training site. The Program Director will complete the appropriate paperwork at this time and send a copy of the paperwork to the counselor.

The Program Director will help the client complete all forms necessary to work at the training site. The Program Director will begin Orientation, explaining hours scheduled to work, job expectations, and when to submit time cards.

Rewrite the first paragraph in a step-by-step list.

Example: Step 1: Counselor will identify _Clients appropriate for program_.

Step 2: Counselor will make a _____ to the Program Director.

Step 3: Program Director will place the client in the _____.

Step 4: Program Director will complete the _____.

Step 5: Program Director will send a _____.

Step 6: During Orientation, the Program Director should explain hours scheduled to work, _____

_____

You are correct if you wrote: 2. *referral*; 3. *appropriate training site*; 4. *appropriate paperwork*; 5. *copy of paperwork to the counselor*; 6. *job expectations, and when to submit time cards.*

Read the following policy and procedures information.

Section U—Resignation

To resign in good standing, an employee shall submit resignation in writing to his/her Director at least two weeks before the effective date of resignation and give his/her reasons therefore. An employee who gives less than two weeks notice without approval of his/her Director shall be subject to discharge.

The employee must receive approval of his/her Director. Director forwards resignation to the Human Resources Director.

All resigning employees are entitled to final evaluation with their Director, the Human Resources Director, and the Executive Director. Request for final evaluations must be made in writing one week before the effective date of resignation.

Upon completion of the requested final evaluations, copies of the evaluations from Director and/or letters of evaluation from Human Resources Director and Executive Director shall be forwarded to Personnel for employee records.

Rewrite the resignation process in a step-by-step list.

Step 1: _____

_____

Step 2: _____

Step 3: _____

Step 4: _____

_____

Step 5: _____

_____

Step 6: If an employee gives less than two weeks notice, what can happen?

_____

. . . .

Reading: Following sequential directions to complete a task; Identifying factual details and specifications within text

MAKING INFERENCES FROM TEXT

Sometimes you need to read a handbook section more than once to understand it.

GUIDED PRACTICE

Read through the *Reasons for Disciplinary Actions* below. Then answer the questions that follow.

---

1.   Gross misconduct, includes but is not limited to:

    a.   assault or threatened assault upon a supervisor, participant or co-worker;

    b.   dishonesty;

    c.   theft;

    d.   arson;

    e.   sabotage;

    f.   damaging agency property through willful negligence; and/or

    g.   drinking on the job or arriving on the job under influence of alcohol or illegal drugs.

2.   Conviction of a felony.

3.   Failure to follow the orders of the Executive Director.

4.   Being absent from work without permission or failure to report to the Human Resources Director when one is absent.

5.   Being habitually absent or tardy.

6.   Failure to perform assigned work in an efficient manner.

7.   Being wasteful of material, property, or working time.

Fill in the reason number that explains why each action is "gross misconduct."

1. Martin took a box of pencils from work and gave it to his son. _____

2. Dixie drank four beers at lunch, and then returned to work. _____

3. Rita told her supervisor that she had turned in a report when she had not. _____

You're correct if you answered: 1. *1c*; 2. *1g*; 3. *1b*.

Using the list of *Reasons for Disciplinary Action* on the previous page, fill in the reason number that explains why each action is "gross misconduct."

Reason   **Action**

1. _____ taking an hour to tell a co-worker about your vacation to the Bahamas

2. _____ telling your manager you have the flu and need to leave early, when you plan to go to a movie matinee

3. _____ not calling in when you have a hangover and miss a day of work

4. _____ spending 10 hours on a report that usually takes 3 hours of work

5. _____ constantly threatening a co-worker just because you don't like him/her personally

6. _____ taking markers from the supply cabinet so your daughter can complete a class project

7. _____ telling your boss you are almost finished with an assignment when you haven't even started

8. _____ without making prior arrangements with your boss, being 15 minutes late every Thursday because you take your son to nursery school.

WORKWISE

Have you ever resigned from a job because you were dissatisfied? Do you know someone who has?

Ask friends and family if they have left a job because they were unhappy. How did they handle the situation? What did they write in their resignation letters? Write down their responses on a separate piece of paper.

WRITE A LETTER USING A POLICY MANUAL

Now use what you've learned about resignation policies to write a letter of resignation. The information you need is listed below. (You would have the letter typed before you submit it to your supervisor.)

- Today's date is April 6. Your last day will be April 20.
- Your supervisor is Mr. Hank Napoli.
- You work at the law firm of Mitchell and Boone, 112 Canal, Lockport, MN 43986
- You are leaving to start another job with the law firm of Townsend, Yosha, and Cline.
- You have worked for Mitchell and Boone for three years.

	home address
person's name and company address	
date	
person's name	
letter	
	Sincerely,
your name	

Purchasing and Selling

Charts and Tables
Verify Sales Tax and Discounts

Product Information for Selling
Use Product Information to Make a Sale

Product Information for Purchasing
Place an Order

CHARTS AND TABLES

Knowing how to read charts and tables is a skill you need in most workplaces. Tables and charts in purchasing and selling use numbers and money amounts.

In the last chapter, you learned how to read rows *across* from left to right and columns *down* from top to bottom. Tables and charts are used often in our everyday lives.

SKILL PREVIEW

How do you get the information you need from tables and charts?

Use the tip table to answer the questions below.

_____ 1. 15% tax on $47

_____ 2. 20% tax on $23

_____ 3. 15% tax on $35

_____ 4. 20% tax on $17

_____ 5. 15% tax on $8

_____ 6. 20% tax on $39

_____ 7. 15% tax on $15

_____ 8. 20% tax on $22

_____ 9. 15% tax on $40

_____ 10. 20% tax on $50

_____ 11. 15% tax on $11

_____ 12. 20% tax on $31

15% & 20% TIP TABLE®

Check	15%	20%	Check	15%	20%
$1.00	$.15	$.20	$26.00	$3.90	$5.20
2.00	.30	.40	27.00	4.05	5.40
3.00	.45	.60	28.00	4.20	5.60
4.00	.60	.80	29.00	4.35	5.80
5.00	.75	1.00	30.00	4.50	6.00
6.00	.90	1.20	31.00	4.65	6.20
7.00	1.05	1.40	32.00	4.80	6.40
8.00	1.20	1.60	33.00	4.95	6.60
9.00	1.35	1.80	34.00	5.10	6.80
10.00	1.50	2.00	35.00	5.25	7.00
11.00	1.65	2.20	36.00	5.40	7.20
12.00	1.80	2.40	37.00	5.55	7.40
13.00	1.95	2.60	38.00	5.70	7.60
14.00	2.10	2.80	39.00	5.85	7.80
15.00	2.25	3.00	40.00	6.00	8.00
16.00	2.40	3.20	41.00	6.15	8.20
17.00	2.55	3.40	42.00	6.30	8.40
18.00	2.70	3.60	43.00	6.45	8.60
19.00	2.85	3.80	44.00	6.60	8.80
20.00	3.00	4.00	45.00	6.75	9.00
21.00	3.15	4.20	46.00	6.90	9.20
22.00	3.30	4.40	47.00	7.05	9.40
23.00	3.45	4.60	48.00	7.20	9.60
24.00	3.60	4.80	49.00	7.35	9.80
25.00	3.75	5.00	50.00	7.50	10.00

FINDING SALES TAX

Most state and local governments have placed a **sales tax** on goods to pay for services provided by those governments. Sometimes, food and medicine are **not taxable**, but almost everything you buy requires a sales tax.

Sales tax is expressed in several ways:

- "so many" cents on a dollar
- a percentage of total sales
- a percentage of taxable sales only

For example, a sale in the amount of $1, with a 5% sales tax would be:

- 5 cents on a dollar = a nickel
- 5% of $1 (total) = a nickel
- 5% of $1 (taxable only) = a nickel

Many sales employees (cashiers, check-out personnel, salesclerks) operate a **point-of-sale** cash register. You may have seen this type of cash register at the grocery store. The salesperson totals the purchases and the point-of-sale cash register finds the tax and the total sale. If a business doesn't have a point-of-sale cash register, it may provide a calculator to figure a sale.   Follow the steps below with a calculator.

GUIDED PRACTICE

Julia Chavez is ringing up a sale of $47.65. The sales tax in her town is 5%. What is the sales tax for $47.65?

ON THE CALCULATOR		
Method A	**Keys**	**Calculator Display**
Step 1: Change a percent to a decimal. 5% = .05		
Step 2: Enter the total on your calculator.	(4)(7)(·)(6)(5)	47.65
Step 3: Enter the multiplication symbol.	(×)	47.65
Step 4: Enter the decimal value for the percent.	(·)(0)(5)	0.05
Step 5: Press the "equals" sign.	(=)	2.3825 rounds to 2.38
The tax is $2.38, so the total cost is $47.65 + $2.38 = $50.03		

You are correct if you found that: *5% of $47.65 is $2.38.*

FINDING TOTAL SALE

In most cases, you need to find the **total sale**, not just the sales tax. You can use this calculator shortcut to find a total. Look at Julia Chavez's sale on page 40.

ON THE CALCULATOR		
Method B	**Keys**	**Calculator Display**
First perform **Steps 1, 2, and 3** as shown on page 40.		(47.65)
Step 4: Enter the number 1.05 (1 represents the total and .05 represents the percent.)	(1) (.) (0) (5)	(1.05)
Step 5: Press the "equals" sign.	(=)	(50.0325) rounds to 50.03
You can round this to $50.03. Is this the same answer as on page 40?		

APPLIED PRACTICE 1: USING SALES TAX

1. Change the following percents to decimals, using the pattern below.
   $7\% = .07$ $25\% = .25$ $6\frac{1}{2}\% = .065$
   a. 3% _____   c. 6% _____   e. $8\frac{1}{2}\%$ _____
   b. $3\frac{1}{2}\%$ _____   d. 8% _____   f. 10% _____

Use a calculator to find the answers for 2 to 4. Use either method shown above. Round your answers to the nearest hundredth.

2. On $12.99 worth of merchandise with a 5% sales tax:
   a. the tax only _____   b. the total sale _____

3. On $1,498 worth of merchandise with a $7\frac{1}{2}\%$ sales tax:
   a. the tax only _____   b. the total sale _____

4. On $547.35 worth of merchandise with a 4% sales tax:
   a. the tax only _____   b. the total sale _____

. . . .
Computation: Performing computations, including calculating sales tax

If you work in retail sales, you use a **fixed-rate tax table** for all sales. This means that the rate does not change. Salespersons use a tax table for quick reference to find the amount of tax to be paid.

Use the sales tax table below to find the tax and the total sale amount for each amount of sale. An example is done for you. (The table is based on a rate of $.08 on the dollar.)

Example:

Amount + Tax(es) = Total Sale
of Sale

4.50 = (4.00 + .50) =
↓   ↓
4.50 + .32 + .04 = $4.86

Sales Tax Table	
Amount of Sale	**Amount of Tax**
$.25	$.02
.50 ⟶	.04
.75	.06
1.00	.08
2.00	.16
3.00	.24
4.00 ⟶	.32
6.00	.48
7.00	.56
8.00	.64
9.00	.72
10.00	.80

1. $6.75 + _____ + _____ = _____

2. $10.25 + _____ + _____ = _____

3. $9.00 + _____ = _____

4. $7.50 + _____ + _____ = _____

5. $17.00 + _____ + _____ = _____
   (*Hint:* This is 10.00 + 7.00)

Invoices are often used for billing people for services and goods they purchased. By using tables, you can complete the mathematical operations needed to fill out invoices quickly and easily.

Shown below is a **multi-rate tax table** used by P&R Printing Company.

Multi-Rate Tax Table										
Quantity	40	41	42	43	44	45	46	47	48	49	50
Price	3.20	3.28	3.36	3.44	3.52	3.60	3.68	3.76	3.84	3.92	4.00
Tax	.26	.26	.27	.27	.28	.28	.29	.30	.31	.32	.32
Total	3.46	3.54	3.63	3.71	3.80	3.88	3.97	4.06	4.15	4.24	4.32

P&R Printing

Miller Mall
244 Main Street
Littletown, AL 36123
(205) 555-1212
FAX (205) 555-0230

Date _____   Number of Copies __47__

SERVICE	QUANTITY	UNIT PRICE	TOTAL
FAX			
Phone Time			
8½ x 11	✓	.08	✓
8½ x 14			
Other			
Collate			
Supplies			
SUB-TOTAL			
TAX			✓
TOTAL			✓

WORLD'S LARGEST PRINTING CHAIN

Part A

Fill in the checked items on the invoice shown above. Use the multi-rate tax table on page 42 to find the price, tax, and total for 47 $8\frac{1}{2}$" × 11" copies made at P&R Printing.

Part B

Use the chart on page 42 to fill in the missing information on the lines below.

1. Quantity __40__ Price _____ Tax _____ Total _____

2. Quantity _____ Price __3.68__ Tax _____ Total _____

3. Quantity _____ Price _____ Tax __27__ Total _____

4. Quantity _____ Price _____ Tax _____ Total __4.32__

5. Quantity __49__ Price _____ Tax _____ Total _____

. . . .
Reading: Reading two or more column charts to obtain information

FIGURING DISCOUNTS

When you use a tax table, you *add on a certain percent* to the sale amount to get the total sale price. But when you figure a **discount**, you *take off* a certain percent from the sale amount to get the discount price.

A discount can be shown in two ways—as a fraction or as a percent: $\frac{1}{2}$ off or 50% off Both mean the same thing even though they are expressed differently.

Many retail stores have point-of-sale cash registers. They discount prices as soon as they are entered. Follow the example below with your own calculator.

Example: $27.95 at 25% discount

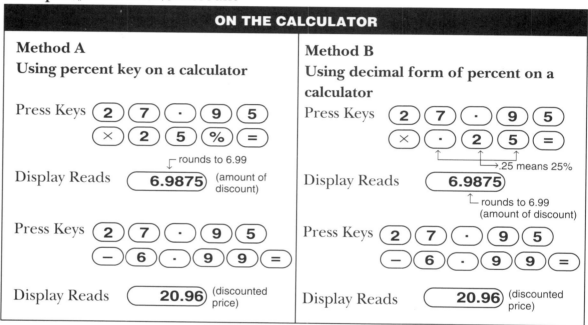

GUIDED PRACTICE

Using a calculator, find the discounted price for the following items. You may use either method A or method B.

1. $13.40 at 25% off = 13.40 × 25% = _____ 13.40 – _____ = _____

2. $24.95 at 50% off = 24.95 × 50% = _____ 24.95 – _____ = _____

3. $57.00 at 30% off = 57.00 × 30% = _____ 57.00 – _____ = _____

You were correct if you found the discounted prices to be: 1. *$10.05*; 2. *$12.48*; and 3. *$39.90.*

Use the **singular sale discount table** to find the discounted prices for the following items. You may have to combine amounts of sale and amounts off, as shown below.

Sale Discount Table		
Amount of Sale	**Amount of Discount**	
	$\frac{1}{4}$ **off**	$\frac{1}{2}$ **off**
$1.00	$.25	$.50
2.00	.50	1.00
3.00	.75	1.50
4.00	1.00	2.00
5.00	1.25	2.50
6.00	1.50	3.00
7.00	1.75	3.50
8.00	2.00	4.00
9.00	2.25	4.50
10.00	2.50	5.00

Example: $17.00 at $\frac{1}{4}$ off or 25% off

Amount of Sale − Amount of Discount = Discounted Price

$$17.00 \quad - (1.75 + 2.50) = 4.25 = 17.00 - 4.25 = 12.75$$

7.00 + 10.00   7.00 + 10.00

1. $13.00 at $\frac{1}{4}$, or 25% off

   13.00 − (_____ + _____) = _____   13.00 − _____ = _____

2. $26.00 at $\frac{1}{2}$, or 50% off

   26.00 − (_____ + _____) = _____   26.00 − _____ = _____

3. $23.00 at $\frac{1}{4}$, or 25% off

   23.00 − (_____ + _____) = _____   23.00 − _____ = _____

4. $18.00 at $\frac{1}{2}$, or 50% off

   18.00 − (_____ + _____) = _____   18.00 − _____ = _____

. . . .
Computation: Performing computations, figuring discounts

Companies sometimes offer a higher discount to customers who pay for their merchandise quickly. They offer a **variable-rate discount** according to how soon the bill is paid. Companies do this so that they will have more cash on hand and so that they will not have to wait as long for customers to pay their bills. Note that on the discount table shown below there is a higher discount if you pay within 10 days than if you pay within 30 days or 60 days.

Discount Table			
Invoice	10-days 10%	30-days 6%	60-days 2%
$ 100.00 500.00 1,000.00 10,000.00	$ 10.00 50.00 100.00 1,000.00	$ 6.00 30.00 60.00 600.00	$ 2.00 10.00 20.00 200.00

Use the discount table to answer the questions.

1. How much would you save your company if you paid for $10,000 worth of merchandise
   a. in 10 days? _____
   b. in 60 days? _____

2. How much would you save your company if you paid for $500 worth of merchandise
   a. in 30 days? _____
   b. in 10 days? _____

3. How much would you save your company if you paid for $1,000 worth of merchandise
   a. in 60 days? _____
   b. in 30 days? _____

4. How much would you save your company if you paid for $100 worth of merchandise
   a. in 10 days? _____
   b. in 30 days? _____

CONVERTING FRACTIONS TO COMPUTE DISCOUNTS

Sometimes discounts are expressed as fractions. It is easier if you convert the fractions to decimals, especially if you are using a calculator. To convert a common fraction to a decimal, divide the **numerator** (top number) by the **denominator** (bottom number). The example shows how to do this on a calculator.

Example: $\frac{5}{8}$ off = $5 \div 8 = .625$

GUIDED PRACTICE

Use a calculator to convert the fractions into decimals. Round your answer to the nearest hundredth.

Fraction   Division   Decimal

1. $\frac{1}{4}$ = ____ ÷ ____ = ____   3. $\frac{3}{4}$ = ____ ÷ ____ = ____

2. $\frac{1}{5}$ = ____ ÷ ____ = ____   4. $\frac{1}{3}$ = ____ ÷ ____ = ____

You are correct if you found that: 1. $\frac{1}{4} = 1 \div 4 = .25$; 2. $\frac{1}{5} = 1 \div 5 = .20$; 3. $\frac{3}{4} = 3 \div 4 = .75$; and 4. $\frac{1}{3} = 1 \div 3 = .33$.

APPLIED PRACTICE 6: COMPUTING DISCOUNTS

Use a calculator to compute the discount to be taken off of each dollar amount. Round your answer to the nearest hundredth.

Example:	$\frac{1}{4}$ off	$\frac{1}{3}$ off	$\frac{1}{2}$ off
$20.00	× .25 = 5.00	× .33 = 6.60	× .50 = 10.00

1. $33.95   _____   _____   _____

2. $17.30   _____   _____   _____

3. $21.50   _____   _____   _____

4. $44.95   _____   _____   _____

VERIFY SALES TAX AND DISCOUNTS

Use the sales tax table to verify the sales tax on each bill.

1.

Abe's Grocery Store	
Cinnamon Squares	2.99
Bob's Bacon	1.99
Kleen-Rite	1.59
Pan's Pizza	1.43
Sub Total	8.00
Tax	.64
Total	8.64

Sales Tax Table	
Amount of Sale	**Amount of Tax**
$.25	$.02
.50 ⟶	.04
.75	.06
1.00	.08
2.00	.16
3.00	.24
4.00 ⟶	.32
6.00	.48
7.00	.56
8.00	.64
9.00	.72
10.00	.80

a. Was the correct sales tax charged?

_____

b. If not, what is the correct sales tax and total?

_____

Power Pharmacy	
Kleenex Tissues	.99
No-Pain Aspirin	2.56
Greeting Card	1.50
Paperback	3.95
Tasty Gum	.50
Sub Total	9.50
Tax	.78
Total	10.28

2. a. Was the correct sales tax charged?

_____

b. If not, what is the correct sales tax and total?

_____

WORKWISE

Find out if the company you work for or a company in your area uses discount tables or sales tax tables. Offer to use what you learned in this chapter to show another student or a co-worker how to use these tables.

PRODUCT INFORMATION FOR SELLING

When you shop for a lamp, tires, or plant food, do you have questions about which brand or price for each item is best? In this lesson, you are a salesperson answering customers' questions and making the sale.

SKILL PREVIEW

Use the following product information to answer a customer's questions.

Sensitive Eyes®
Saline Solution

DIRECTIONS FOR USE:
Rinsing After Cleaning
• After cleaning, thoroughly rinse lenses with **Sensitive Eyes** Saline Solution.

Heat (thermal) Disinfection
• Use fresh **Sensitive Eyes** Saline Solution when heat disinfecting. Follow the directions provided with your disinfecting unit.

Chemical Disinfection (including Hydrogen Peroxide Systems)
• Following disinfection, rinse lenses thoroughly with **Sensitive Eyes** Saline Solution before insertion.

Protein Removal
• Use **Sensitive Eyes** Saline Solution to dissolve enzymatic cleaning tablets.
• Follow directions provided with the enzymatic cleaner.

Sensitive Eyes®
Saline Solution

To maintain your soft contact lenses in their best possible condition and for better wearing comfort, Bausch & Lomb recommends that you use Sensitive Eyes Saline Solution in conjunction with Sensitive Eyes Daily Cleaner, Sensitive Eyes Drops and Sensitive Eyes Enzymatic Cleaner.

PRECAUTIONS:
• Never re-use this solution.
• Keep the bottle tightly closed when not in use.
• Store at room temperature.
• Use before the expiration date marked on the carton and bottle.

WARNING:
SEE PACKAGE INSERT FOR IMPORTANT SAFETY INFORMATION.

---

1. "What is the trademark (brand name) of the product?" _____

2. "I'm allergic to hydrogen peroxide. Can I use this solution?" _____

3. "Can I reuse this saline solution?" _____

4. "Can I use this solution with my enzymatic cleaner?" _____

UNDERSTANDING PRODUCT INFORMATION

Why should you know product information as a salesperson? Often customers will ask you:

- *Which* product is the best and why?
- *How* and *when* should I use the product?
- *What* special precautions should I take when I use or store the product?

You can find information about a product on the label, box, or special manual (booklet) that comes with the product. Labels often print key words in **bold** or colored type, or use pictures to show how to use a product. Sometimes a customer wants to hear and read information before spending money on a product. While pointing to the label, box, or booklet, you can answer the customer's questions with confidence and send another satisfied buyer on his or her way.

GUIDED PRACTICE

Read the product label to answer the customer's questions.

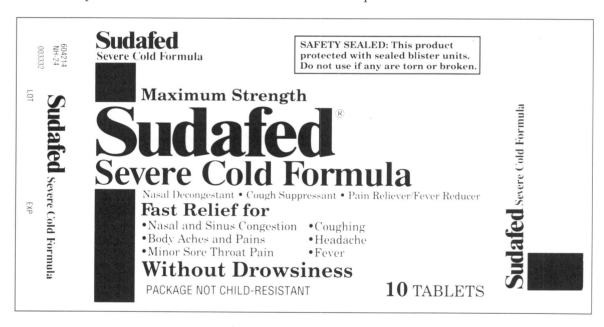

1. "What is the brand name of the product?"_____
   (You've started out right if you wrote *Sudafed Severe Cold Formula.*)

2. "How many symptoms does this cold formula relieve?"_____
   (If you counted *6 symptoms,* you are right.)

3. "Will Sudafed relieve my sore throat pain and coughing?"_____
   (If you look at the symptoms listed, the answer is *yes.*)

Product information comes in many forms. Usually the product labels, boxes, or pamphlets (booklets) read from top to bottom and from left to right. Use the product label to answer the customer's questions.

SUPER K-GRO PLANT FOOD
LIQUID FERTILIZER — JUST MIX WITH WATER
Convenient measuring spoon included in package.

Apply SUPER K-GRO solution liberally around plant roots. Soak soil out as far as branches extend. Spray or sprinkle leaves of outdoor plants for fast foliar feeding. Use a clean sprinkling can, pail or SUPER K-GRO Hose End Sprayer.

Plant Food Storage. SUPER K-GRO plant food is water soluble and will absorb moisture, and in certain climates it will harden in storage. This hardening does nothing to diminish the effectiveness of SUPER K-GRO. Simply break up large lumps with a dull tool. Mixed with water, even very hard lumps will dissolve.

FEEDING DIRECTIONS
HOUSEPLANTS. One TEAspoon per gallon of water. Soak plant soil every two to four weeks. (Leaf feeding is not recommended.)
LAWNS. One tablespoon per gallon of water for every 25 sq. ft. Apply every two weeks.
TREES. Fruit and Ornamental. One tablespoon per gallon of water for every 10 sq. ft. Soak soil out as far as branches extend. Feed three times a year — April, June, July.
EVERGREENS. Needle and Broadleaf types. One tablespoon per gallon of water for every 10 sq. ft. Apply every two weeks.
DECIDUOUS SHRUBS. (Drops leaves in winter). One tablespoon per gallon of water for every 15 sq. ft. Apply every two weeks.
TOMATOES. One tablespoon per gallon of water for every plant. Apply every two weeks.
BERRIES. (Including other small fruit) One tablespoon per gallon of water for every 10 sq. ft. Apply every three to four weeks.
ROSES. Large bushes over 2 ft. wide. One tablespoon per gallon of water per bush. Apply every two weeks.
ROSES. Smaller bushes under 2 ft. wide. One-half to one tablespoon per gallon of water per bush. Apply every two weeks.
ALL OTHER FLOWERS & VEGETABLES. One tablespoon per gallon of water for every 10 sq. ft. Apply every two weeks.

1. "Should I mix Super K-Gro with anything before I apply it?"

   _____

2. "Where should I apply Super K-Gro?" _____

3. "What are the feeding directions for tomatoes?" _____

   _____

4. "Will this product help my rosebushes?" _____

5. "What should I do if the plant food hardens in storage?"

   _____

6. "How often should I use Super K-Gro on my lawn?" _____

7. "Should I feed the leaves on my houseplants?" _____

. . . .
Reading: Identifying factual details and specifications within text

EXPLAINING PRODUCTS

Some customers need more convincing than others. They want to know what the benefits of a product are. You, as the salesperson, have to pay particular attention to:

- *who* the buyer is
- *what* the buyer is looking for
- *what* is the most important product feature to the buyer

GUIDED PRACTICE

Use the back panel to find answers to the customer's questions. Note the words in **bold print** draw attention to product information.

Only the Sudafed® brand name on your purchase assures that this product was manufactured by Burroughs Wellcome Co.
Our heritage is our commitment to excellence.

©1991
BURROUGHS WELLCOME CO.
Research Triangle Park, NC 27709
Made in U.S.A.

PRODUCT BENEFITS: Maximum allowable levels of nasal decongestant, cough suppressant, and non-aspirin pain reliever/fever reducer provide temporary relief from symptoms of the common cold and flu. This product contains no ingredients that may cause drowsiness. The **DECONGESTANT** (pseudoephedrine) temporarily relieves nasal and sinus congestion due to the common cold. It temporarily relieves nasal stuffiness; reduces the swelling of nasal passages; shrinks swollen membranes; and temporarily restores freer breathing through the nose. The **COUGH SUPPRESSANT** (dextromethorphan) temporarily relieves cough due to the common cold. The non-aspirin **PAIN RELIEVER/FEVER REDUCER** (acetaminophen) temporarily relieves headache, body aches and pains, minor sore throat pain, and reduces fever due to the common cold.

DIRECTIONS: Adults and children 12 years of age and over, 2 tablets every 6 hours, not to exceed 8 tablets in 24 hours. Not recommended for children under 12 years of age.

EACH TABLET CONTAINS: acetaminophen 500 mg, dextromethorphan hydrobromide 15 mg, and pseudoephedrine hydrochloride 30 mg. Also contains: crospovidone, magnesium stearate, microcrystalline cellulose, povidone, pregelatinized corn starch, sodium starch glycolate and stearic acid.

WARNINGS: Do not exceed recommended dosage because at higher doses nervousness, dizziness, or sleeplessness may occur. Do not take this product for more than 10 days. A persistent cough may be a sign of a serious condition. If cough persists for more than 7 days, tends to recur, or is accompanied by rash, persistent headache, fever that lasts for more than 3 days, or if new symptoms occur, consult a physician. Do not take this product for persistent or chronic cough such as occurs with smoking, asthma, emphysema, or if cough is accompanied by excessive phlegm (mucus) unless directed by a physician. If sore throat is severe, persists for more than 2 days, is accompanied or followed by fever, headache, rash, nausea, or vomiting, consult a physician promptly. Do not take this product if you have high blood pressure, heart disease, diabetes, thyroid disease, or difficulty in urination due to enlargement of the prostate gland except under the advice and supervision of a physician. As with any drug, if you are pregnant or nursing a baby, seek the advice of a health professional before using this product.

Drug Interaction Precaution: Do not take this product if you are presently taking a prescription antihypertensive or antidepressant drug containing a monoamine oxidase inhibitor except under the advice and supervision of a physician.

KEEP THIS AND ALL DRUGS OUT OF THE REACH OF CHILDREN. In case of accidental overdose, seek professional assistance or contact a Poison Control Center immediately. Prompt medical attention is critical for adults as well as for children even if you do not notice any signs or symptoms.

Store at 15° to 25°C (59° to 77°F) in a dry place.

N 3   0081-0773-13   3

- Knowing *what* about the product is knowing the **product feature.**

1. "How many milligrams (mg) of acetaminophen does each tablet contain?" _____
   (The correct answer is *500 mg.*)

2. "At what temperature should Sudafed Severe Cold Formula be stored? _____
   (You are correct if you answered *15° to 25°C.*)

   - Knowing *how* the product can benefit a customer is knowing the **product benefits.**

3. "What is the first product benefit listed?" _____
   (The correct answer comes after PRODUCT BENEFITS—*nasal decongestant*)

A product benefit can be a valuable piece of information. For example, another benefit of Sudafed Severe Cold Formula is that it is a non-aspirin pain reliever and fever reducer.

- Knowing *who* buys the product is knowing the **target audience.**

4. "Will Sudafed Severe Cold Formula relieve my cough and fever?"
   Yes, because it contains a _____
   (You are correct if you wrote *cough suppressant and non-aspirin pain reliever/fever reducer.*)

5. "What is the dosage direction for adults?" _____
   (The correct answer is *2 tablets every 6 hours, not to exceed 8 tablets in 24 hours.*)

APPLIED PRACTICE 2: IDENTIFYING TARGET AUDIENCE

Use the product label to complete the statement.

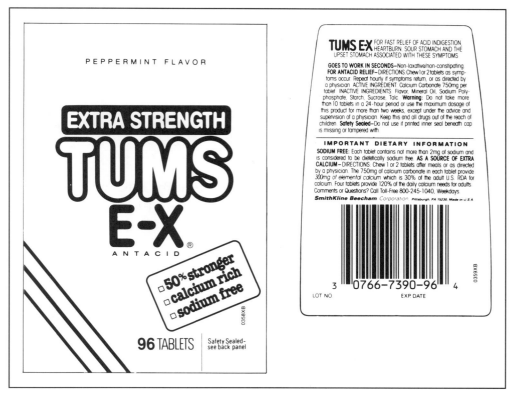

I would sell this product to an adult with the following symptoms:

1. *heartburn* _____   3. _____

2. _____   4. _____

. . . .

Reading: Identifying factual details and specifications within text; Following sequential directions to complete a task.

IDENTIFYING DETAILS ABOUT PRODUCTS

Brochures, catalogs, charts, and pictures give details about products. In the brochure below, the **details** (product name, finish, product features, and cost) are labeled for the first type of paint. Use the brochure to answer the questions.

Product Name →

Finish →

Product Features →

Cost →

Lucite 8 Year Interior Flat Latex Paint
• 8 year warranty
• Soap and water washability
7⁹⁹ 1 Gallon
Semi-Gloss ..10.99

Lucite Flat 12 Year Latex Interior Paint
• 12 year warranty
• One-coat coverage
• Splatter resistant
11⁹⁹ 1 Gallon
Semi-Gloss ..14.99

Dura-Color™ 12 Year Flat Interior Latex
• Applies easily, dries quickly
• One coat coverage
12⁹⁹ 1 Gallon
Semi-Gloss ..15.99
Satin 15.99

Lucite 8 Year Exterior Flat Latex Paint
• 8 year warranty
• Easy clean-up
• White only
9⁹⁹ 1 Gallon

Lucite 12 Year Flat Exterior Latex Paint
• Resists cracking and peeling
• Mica-fortified
14⁹⁹ 1 Gallon

Pittsburgh Floor & Porch Flat Latex
• Excellent durability
• No-scuff finish
• Easy clean-up
14⁹⁹ 1 Gallon

Dura-Color™ 12 Year Flat Exterior Latex
• Resists cracking and peeling
• Mildew-resistant
16⁹⁹ 1 Gallon

1. Is the Lucite Flat 12 Year Latex paint for interior use, exterior use, or both? _____ (You were right if you said *both*–the second and fifth.)

2. What type of finish does the Pittsburgh Floor & Porch Flat Latex paint have? _____ (You could have answered *flat* or *no-scuff finish*.)

Use the brochure to answer the questions.

1. Lucite 8 Year Interior Latex paint comes in _____ or _____ finish and costs _____ or _____ per gallon.

2. Dura-Color 12 Year Flat Exterior Latex paint resists _____ and _____ and costs _____ per gallon.

3. Pittsburgh Floor & Porch paint has a flat, _____ finish and costs _____ per gallon.

Use the product label to answer questions about the product's key features.

NDC 0031-8624-12   4 FL. OZ.

Robitussin®
(GUAIFENESIN SYRUP, USP)

EXPECTORANT

DIRECTIONS: Follow dosage below:
Do Not Exceed Recommended Dosage.
ADULT DOSE (and children 12 years and over): 2–4 teaspoonfuls every 4 hours.
CHILD DOSE
6 years to under 12 years:
1–2 teaspoonfuls every 4 hours.
2 years to under 6 years:
½–1 teaspoonful every 4 hours.
Under 2—Consult Your Doctor.

TAMPER-EVIDENT BOTTLE CAP.
IF BREAKABLE RING IS
SEPARATED, DO NOT USE.

WARNINGS: A persistent cough may be a sign of a serious condition. If cough persists for more than 1 week, tends to recur, or is accompanied by fever, rash, or persistent headache, consult a doctor. Do not take this product for persistent or chronic cough such as occurs with smoking, asthma, chronic bronchitis, emphysema, or if cough is accompanied by excessive phlegm (mucus) unless directed by a doctor. As with any drug, if you are pregnant or nursing a baby, seek the advice of a health professional before using this product.

KEEP THIS AND ALL DRUGS OUT OF REACH OF CHILDREN. IN CASE OF ACCIDENTAL OVERDOSE, SEEK PROFESSIONAL ASSISTANCE OR CONTACT A POISON CONTROL CENTER IMMEDIATELY.

INDICATIONS: Expectorant action to help loosen phlegm and thin bronchial secretions to make coughs more productive.

Active Ingredients per teaspoonful (5 mL)
Guaifenesin, USP 100 mg in pleasant tasting syrup with alcohol 3.5 percent.

Store at Controlled Room Temperature, Between 15°C and 30°C (59°F and 86°F).

CONSUMER PRODUCTS DIVISION
A. H. ROBINS COMPANY, RICHMOND, VA. 23230

7.89

1. "What is the name of the product?" _____

2. "What percentage of alcohol does the product contain?" _____

3. "Is this an expectorant or a suppressant?" _____

4. "The ring seal on the bottle is broken. Should I use this?" _____

5. "I am three months pregnant. Should I use this product?"_____

Answer the next two questions as if you were selling this product to a 25-year-old woman who has an 8-year-old son.

6. "My son and I both have a cough and the flu. Our doctor recommended this product. What dosage should I take?" _____

7. "What dosage should I give my son?" _____

EXPLAINING A PRODUCT

As a salesperson, you might use the brochure to sell tires to customers. Knowing the product details will help you make the sale.

You need to be prepared to answer the following questions:

- *What* is the product?
- *How much* does it cost?
- *What* are the product's features?
- *How* do the features and benefits help the customer?

Use the information in the tire brochure to fill in the blanks as if you were explaining features and benefits of the Sportiva EM4 tire.

GENERAL TIRE Ⓖ

SPORTIVA EM4

An outstanding European designed metric performer—at an affordable price.

It is European engineered for outstanding handling and cornering. Designed to look as good as it performs. Available in metric sizes for many imported sport sedans. And affordably priced to give you more for your money.
   Meet the Sportiva EM4: a tire that brings international performance and style to the American road.

Made for the value-conscious enthusiast.

FEATURES	CUSTOMER BENEFITS
"T" Speed Rated*	■ Rated for speeds of up to 118 mph.
Specially Designed Shoulder Contour	■ For outstanding handling and cornering.
Computer Designed Tread	■ For optimum traction and braking.
Refined Tread Compound	■ Designed to deliver excellent mileage.
Center Stabilizing Rib	■ Directional stability and steering control.
Mud & Snow Rated	■ For all-season performance.
Metric Sizing	■ Sizes to fit many imported sport sedans.

To begin your sales statement, you name the product. "This is the _____." (You are right on track if you said *Sportiva EM4*.)

You continue with a brief description of the tire found under the title. "The Sportiva EM4 is an outstanding European designed _____

_____ ."

(When you wrote *metric performer—at an affordable price,* you were right again.)

Now you need to ask what the customer wants out of the tire. This is where you match the product feature with how it will benefit the customer. The customer might say: "I want a tire for my sports sedan that will give me great mileage." You can look at the Features/Customer Benefits part of the brochure and say: "The Sportiva EM4 features a refined tread compound. It is designed to _____." (You are right if you said *deliver excellent mileage*.)

You might close your sales talk with the customer by saying: "Most important, the Sportiva EM4 is made for the _____." (You are right if you wrote *value-conscious enthusiast*.)

APPLIED PRACTICE 5: RELATING PRODUCT FEATURES AND BENEFITS

John Thompson walks in the door, picks up the tire brochure, and walks toward you. As he hands you the brochure, he says, "Tell me a little about this tire." You ask him what he wants out of a tire and he explains.

"I am a salesman on the road all year in all kinds of weather. Living here in Brighton, I have to keep control of my car on some very tight winding curves. I also want tires with the kind of tread that will allow me to brake suddenly if I need to."

Identify the customer's two needs in a tire. Use the tire brochure to match the two features and customer benefits that will satisfy this customer most.

What the Customer Wants in a Tire

1. _____

2. _____

Features   **Customer Benefits**

3. _____   _____

   _____   _____

4. _____   _____

   _____   _____

WORKWISE

Go to a tire store and walk in as a customer. Find a tire brochure and ask a salesperson about the tire. Ask about tire features and benefits, cost, and warranty. Then write down the salesperson's responses.

. . . .
Writing: Recording essential information that involves more than one sentence

USE PRODUCT INFORMATION TO MAKE A SALE

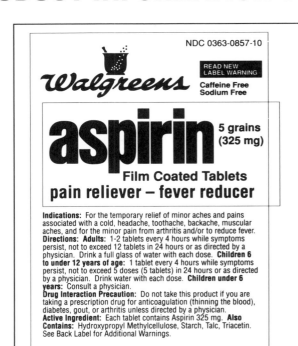

WARNINGS: Children and teenagers should not use this medicine for chicken pox or flu symptoms before a doctor is consulted about Reye Syndrome, a rare but serious illness reported to be associated with aspirin. Do not take this product for pain for more than 10 days (for adults) or 5 days (for children), and do not take for fever for more than 3 days unless directed by a physician. If pain or fever persists or gets worse, if new symptoms occur, or if redness or swelling is present, consult a physician because these could be signs of a serious condition. Do not give this product to children for the pain of arthritis unless directed by a physician. Do not take this product if you are allergic to aspirin or if you have asthma unless directed by a physician. If ringing in the ears or a loss of hearing occurs, consult a physician before taking any more of this product. Do not take this product if you have stomach problems (such as heartburn, upset stomach, or stomach pain) that persists or recur, or if you have ulcers or bleeding problems, unless directed by a physician. As with any drug, if you are pregnant or nursing a baby, seek the advice of a health professional before using this product. IT IS ESPECIALLY IMPORTANT NOT TO USE ASPIRIN DURING THE LAST 3 MONTHS OF PREGNANCY UNLESS SPECIFICALLY DIRECTED TO DO SO BY A DOCTOR BECAUSE IT MAY CAUSE PROBLEMS IN THE UNBORN CHILD OR COMPLICATIONS DURING DELIVERY. KEEP THIS AND ALL DRUGS OUT OF THE REACH OF CHILDREN. IN CASE OF ACCIDENTAL OVERDOSE, SEEK PROFESSIONAL ASSISTANCE OR CONTACT A POISON CONTROL CENTER IMMEDIATELY.
Sodium Free (less than 5 mg. sodium per adult dose of 2 tablets). Keep tightly closed.
Dist.: Walgreen Co., Deerfield, IL 60015

W73403

Dominique Wilson comes into the store where you work. Dominique works full-time, is a single parent, and has two children. Dominique has to spend her money wisely. She shows you a bottle of Walgreen's Aspirin. She asks, "Are there any warnings I should know about before my children and I use this product?"

Read the WARNINGS section on the aspirin label. What are four questions you could ask her before you recommend this brand of aspirin?

1. _____

2. _____

3. _____

4. _____

5. On a separate sheet of paper, write a brief product description of Walgreen's Aspirin. Include the product features, benefits, and dosage for children and adults.

PRODUCT INFORMATION FOR PURCHASING

Budgeting is one way of knowing if you have enough money to buy the food and household items you need. At work, you might have the same responsibility to order and purchase supplies or materials within a budget.

SKILL PREVIEW

You work in the accounting department at ACE Super Supply. Use the supply catalog excerpt from Decker's and the information below to complete the purchase order on page 161. Make a Xerox, so you can reuse this form.

- Fill in the address for Decker's. (See page 65.)
- Ship to your address at ACE Super Supply. It is 841 Rhodes, Rm. 402, Anaheim, CA 90001.
- Date required: September 20.
- Ship via U.P.S. (United Parcel Service)
- Terms: C.O.D. (cash on delivery)
- Fill in the total price for 40 red Sanford Sharpie Markers ($40 \times .60 =$ sale price).
- Order 30 green Sanford Sharpie Markers. Fill in the prices.
- Sign your name as the purchasing agent.

◾SANFORD®

SHARPIE® MARKERS
Permanent marker with quick drying, high intensity ink. Fine point. 12/BX.

NO.	COLOR
30001	Black
30002	Red
30003	Blue
30004	Green

LIST $0.99 Ea. **SALE $0.60** Ea.

IDENTIFYING APPROPRIATE PRODUCT ADS

At the local library or your workplace, you can find most product ads in

- newspapers
- company brochures
- catalogs
- trade magazines

Many businesses publish **trade magazines** that advertise product and service information about their industry. For instance, *Popular Photography* magazine includes ads from various companies about lenses, filters, types of film, and cameras. They often compare products, prices, benefits, and drawbacks.

GUIDED PRACTICE

Match each part of the ad with its correct label below. Write the letter on the line.

1. product description (name) _____

2. product specifications (details) _____

3. quantity included _____

4. price per unit (cost for *one* item) _____

5. ways to order _____

6. terms (how to make payment) _____

7. To place an order you would call toll-free _____.

8. To get more information before you order you would call _____.

You are correct if you matched: 1. *c*; 2. *e*; 3. *d*; 4. *f*; 5. *a*; 6. *b*; 7. *(800) 221-2253*; 8. *(212) 675-8600*

Use the information on the previous page to complete each statement.

1. Two places where you can find product ads are at
   a. _____ or b. _____.

2. You can find most ads in:
   a. _____   c. _____
   b. _____   d. _____

3. Trade magazines advertise _____ and _____ information about their industry.

You work for a lawn care company. You want to order the new Weed Wizard. Match each numbered part of the ad with its correct label. Write the letters on the line.

_____ 1. order form

_____ 2. how to order

_____ 3. terms

_____ 4. product name

_____ 5. product details

_____ 6. price per unit

a → THE NEW! **Weed Wizard.**

e → ONLY **$21⁹⁵**

b ↘ TO ORDER CALL TODAY **1-800-262-5122** (Call for dealership inquiry)

d → *the amazing new solution to rotary trimmer line problems*
- No more trouble with trimmer line — **never buy line again!**
- Easy to install on **your** gas trimmer.
- Cuts through tough weeds, briars and grass.
- Keeps **your** rotary trimmer in business.
- **Guaranteed** to save you time!

c → ✂ -
( ) VISA ( ) M/C #_____ Exp. Date_____
( ) Check enclosed for $21.95 plus $3.00 postage and handling.   MEN 892

Your Trimmer Make _____ Model #_____
Name _____ Phone (____)_____
f → Street _____
City _____ State _____ Zip _____
g → Send to: **WEED WIZARD, INC.,** P.O. Box 275, Dahlonega, Georgia 30533

· · · · · · · · · · · ·
Reading: Identifying factual details and specifications within text

COMPARING ADVERTISING FOR VARIOUS PRODUCTS

You've heard the expression, "It's only money." However, at work, purchasing within a budget is an important business practice. Getting the best product for the least amount of money is very important. But buying the cheapest product does not always mean you are buying the best product for your needs.

When comparing product information:

- Identify what purpose you need the product for.
- List the product features of each product you want to purchase and match those features to your needs.
- Compare the cost to the number of features.

GUIDED PRACTICE

You need to buy a calculator for the accounting department.

Step 1: Using the catalog excerpts below, fill in the chart for each calculator.

> **7.** Canon Print/Display Calculator P20DX.
> 10-digit print. LCD display. 2¼" paper.
> Includes adapter or uses 4 AA batts.* 2 lbs.
> ★★P20DXRCN (1VAC) **$29.97**............ $34.95†
> **8.** Texas Instruments Desktop Print/Display
> Calculator TI5029. 10-digit print, LED.
> Includes AC adapter or 4 AA batts.* 3 lbs.
> ★★5029RTX (1VAC) **$29.97**................ $34.95†
> **9.** Royal EZVue Printing Calculator Model
> 550HD. Extra large 10-digit LCD display. AC
> adapter, paper included. 4 AA batts.* 3 lbs.
> ★★550RY (1VAC) **Your Cost $32.84**... $36.95†

	Product 7	**Product 8**	**Product 9**
A. name	_____	_____	_____
B. type of print	_____	_____	_____
C. type of display	_____	_____	_____
D. batteries/adapter	_____	_____	_____
E. weight	_____	_____	_____
F. cost	_____	_____	_____

You are correct if you answered: 7. a. *Canon Print/Display Calculator P20DX*, b. *10-digit*, c. *LCD*, d. *both*, e. *2 lbs.*, f. *$29.97*; 8. a. *Texas Instruments Desktop Print/Display Calculator TI5029*, b. *10-digit*, c. *LED*, d. *both*, e. *3 lbs.*, f. *$29.97*; 9. a. *Royal EZVue Printing Calculator Model 550HD*, b. *extra large 10-digit*, c. *LCD*, d. *both*, e. *3 lbs.*, f. *$32.84.*

Step 2: Compare the three calculator feature lists on the previous page to your needs listed below. You have a $40 budget.

- You do most of your work in your office and not at home.
- You have found Royal products reliable.
- You work with numbers all day and don't want eye strain.
- You need an adapter.

Choose the calculator from page 62 that would best meet your needs.

1. I would order the _____.

2. The model number is _____.

3. The order number is _____.

You are correct if you answered: 1. *Royal EZVue Calculator*; 2. *550HD*; 3. *550RY*.

APPLIED PRACTICE 3: COMPARING AD INFORMATION ON A GIVEN PRODUCT

You are the office manager. You need to order a typewriter for a new secretary.

Step 1: On a separate sheet of paper, list the product features of each Smith Corona typewriter shown below.

5. Smith Corona Electronic Typewriter Model SL570. 75,000-word Spell-Right® dictionary with WordFind®. Full-line correction memory with word and line eraser. Auto return, center, underscore and bold print. Triple pitch. Auto page insert. 14 lbs. ★SL570CM (2VAC) **$139.97**............... $149.95†	**10. Smith Corona Word Processing Typewriter Model SD670.** 7,000-word editable memory, 16-character display, battery backup, full-line memory correction, and 75,000-word Spell-Right® dictionary. Provides alternatives for misspelled words with Word-Right®/AutoSpell®. Includes correcting cassette. 15 lbs. ★SD670CM (2VAC) **$169.97**............. $189.95†

Step 2: You have a $150 budget. Compare your product feature lists to these needs.

- full-line memory correction
- auto return
- Spell-Right
- WordFind

Choose the typewriter that would best meet the secretary's needs.

1. I would order the _____ typewriter.

2. The model number is _____.

3. The order number is _____.

. . . .
Reading: Identifying similarities and differences in objects

FILLING OUT A PURCHASE ORDER

As an employee of a company, you need to provide **documentation** of what you want to order, get approval, and then place the order. **Purchase orders** are documentation that an order has been approved and is being placed. **Vendors** are the companies that sell goods (products) or services.

Use the contents of the purchase order to answer the questions.

```
                    PURCHASE ORDER                          3785

TO
    Green's Greenhouse Supplies
ADDRESS
        422 W. Arbor Rd., Fremont, NE    68025
SHIP TO
    Flower Fashions
ADDRESS
    1022 Harrison, Dunkirk, MO    34317

REQ. NO.              FOR                        DATE
    55771             C. Wallace/Arrangement       7-25-93
DATE REQUIRED  HOW SHIP                          TERMS Acct.#204
  8-1-93       U.P.S.                                  30 Days
```

QUANTITY	PLEASE SUPPLY ITEMS LISTED BELOW	PRICE		UNIT
1	100	Rolls of green tape (1 box)	35	00	.35
2	5	Yards of 2" white ribbon	50	00	10—
3	30	White pipe cleaners (3 boxes)	9	00	3—
4					

IMPORTANT

OUR ORDER NUMBER MUST APPEAR ON ALL INVOICES-PACKAGES, ETC.

PLEASE NOTIFY US IMMEDIATELY IF YOU ARE UNABLE TO SHIP COMPLETE ORDER BY DATE SPECIFIED.

PLEASE SEND **3** COPIES OF YOUR INVOICE

Caroline Wallace

PURCHASING AGENT

1. The purchase order number is ____ ____ ____ ____.

2. The requisition number for this order is ____ ____ ____ ____ ____.

3. The terms are that the order is to be paid within ____ days.

4. The order is placed *to*_____.

You are right if you answered: 1. *3785*; 2. *55771*; 3. *30*; 4. *Green's Greenhouse Supplies*.

Use the catalog information below to fill in the following purchase order form.

You need: 3 boxes 6" × 9" clasp envelopes
3 boxes 9" × 12" clasp envelopes
2 boxes $4\frac{1}{8}$" × $9\frac{1}{2}$" white commercial envelopes

- Order goes to Decker's, 19 W. 9th St., Anderson, IN 46015.
- Ship to your workplace: MRT Marketing Co., One Mills Road, Bedford, WA 70770.
- Req. No. 349
- For: Mailing Dept.
- Today's date: April 3; date required: April 10
- Ship via U.P.S.; terms: C.O.D.
- 4 copies of their invoice to be sent back to you
- Sign your name as the purchasing agent.

QUALITY PARK COMMERCIAL ENVELOPES

Finest quality bright white envelopes. 500 per box.

NO.	SIZE	TYPE	LIST	SALE
10312	3⅝" x 6½"	6¾	$12.30 Bx.	$6.19 Bx.
11112	4⅛" x 9½"	10	14.06 Bx.	6.39 Bx.

WINDOW ENVELOPES

20212	3⅝" x 6½"	6¾	$14.60 Bx.	$6.79 Bx.
21312	4⅛" x 9½"	10	16.22 Bx.	8.59 Bx.

QUALITY PARK CLASP ENVELOPES

Clasp envelopes have heavily gummed flaps and extra-wide seams. 28# stock. 100 per box.

NO.	SIZE	LIST	SALE
37855	6" x 9"	$11.00 Bx.	$4.99 Bx.
37890	9" x 12"	14.32 Bx.	6.49 Bx.
37897	10" x 13"	16.80 Bx.	7.49 Bx.
37898	10" x 15"	19.64 Bx.	9.00 Bx.
37910	12" x 15½"	26.96 Bx.	10.29 Bx.

PURCHASE ORDER 3754

TO

ADDRESS

SHIP TO

ADDRESS

REQ. NO.	FOR	DATE
DATE REQUIRED	HOW SHIP	TERMS

QUANTITY	PLEASE SUPPLY ITEMS LISTED BELOW	PRICE	UNIT
1			
2			
3			
4			
5			
6			
7			
8			
9			

IMPORTANT

OUR ORDER NUMBER MUST APPEAR ON ALL INVOICES-PACKAGES, ETC.

PLEASE NOTIFY US IMMEDIATELY IF YOU ARE UNABLE TO SHIP COMPLETE ORDER BY DATE SPECIFIED.

PLEASE SEND   COPIES OF YOUR INVOICE

PURCHASING AGENT

Writing: Entering appropriate information onto a form

COMPARING COSTS AGAINST A BUDGET

Spending under your budget is a good business practice. You should know what your budget is before you start comparing products to make a purchase.

GUIDED PRACTICE

The **cost** of a product should reflect the value of the product. When you are comparing the cost of a product, pay special attention to the product features.

You have budgeted $25 for pens. You need to order pens at $1.05 per box (10 pens per box). The **cost per unit** in this example is $1.05 (unit = box). The **unit count** is 10 pens.

Use the following formula to calculate what you can purchase and still stay within your budget:

budget   cost per unit = total # of units to order

$25   ÷ $1.05   =   _____

So, using the information above, divide $25 by $1.05. You may use a calculator.

(2)(5)(÷)(1)(·)(0)(5)(=) _____ boxes.

You are correct if you have the answer: *23.8*; but, you can purchase *23 full boxes*.

To calculate the total **quantity** of pens: total # of units × unit count = quantity

23 units   ×   10 pens   = 230 pens

Practice calculating and filling in the missing information:

Budget	÷	Cost/unit	=	Total # of units	×	Unit Ct.	=	Quantity
1. $40		$3.50		_____		14		_____
2. $10		$.15		_____		12		_____
3. $100		$7.89		_____		5		_____

You are correct if you wrote: 1. *11, 154*; 2. *66, 792*; 3. *12, 60*.

Use a calculator to fill in the missing information.

Budget	÷ Cost/Unit	= Total # of Units	× Unit Ct.	= Quantity
1. $125	$23.50	_____	5	_____
2. $35	$4.10	_____	10	_____
3. $96	$.30	_____	100	_____
4. $75	$11.99	_____	1	_____
5. $59	$7.17	_____	5	_____
6. $10	$1.50	_____	10	_____

WORKWISE

Go to the magazine section of a local library. Ask a librarian to help you find two trade magazines that relate to your current career or career goal. In the space provided below, write and list

- the title of the trade magazine
- three product or service ads from which you could place an order

1. Magazine _____

   Product/Service a. _____

   b. _____

   c. _____

2. Magazine _____

   Product/Service a. _____

   b. _____

   c. _____

. . . .
Computation: Calculating costs and cost savings

PLACE AN ORDER

Use the office supply ad and the following information to complete the purchase order on page 161. You may use a calculator.

- Send to Decker's, 19 W. 9th St., Anderson, IN 46015.
- Ship to your workplace: 1st National Bank, 1313 Madison Street, Toledo, OH 48806.
- Requisition #9099; for: Loan Dept.; date: March 4
- Date required: March 5; ship via Federal Express overnight; terms: C.O.D.
- Order 50 green 3" × 3" Post-it Notes. List the price per unit and the total price. Order 100 cream 4" × 6" Post-it Notes and list the prices for those.
- Have 3 copies sent to you. Sign your name as the purchasing agent.

3M **POST-IT™ NOTES**
Versatile self-stick notes.

NO.	SIZE	COLOR	LIST	SALE
653-YW	1 1/2" x 2"	Yellow	$5.56 Pk	$3.59 Pk.
656-BE	2" x 3"	Blue	0.78 Pd.	0.55 Pd.
656-GN	2" x 3"	Green	0.78 Pd.	0.55 Pd.
656-PK	2" x 3"	Pink	0.78 Pd.	0.55 Pd.
656-YW	2" x 3"	Yellow	0.78 Pd.	0.50 Pd.
654-BE	3" x 3"	Blue	1.07 Pd.	0.75 Pd.
654-GN	3" x 3"	Green	1.07 Pd.	0.75 Pd.
654-PK	3" x 3"	Pink	1.07 Pd.	0.75 Pd.
654-YW	3" x 3"	Yellow	1.07 Pd.	0.69 Pd.
657-YW	3" x 4"	Yellow	1.24 Pd.	0.80 Pd.
655-YW	3" x 5"	Yellow	1.38 Pd.	0.89 Pd.
659-YW	4" x 6"	Yellow	2.13 Pd.	1.39 Pd.
660-CM*	4" x 6"	Cream	2.24 Pd.	1.59 Pd.
660-GY*	4" x 6"	Lt. Gray	2.24 Pd.	1.59 Pd.
660-YW*	4" x 6"	Yellow	2.24 Pd.	1.45 Pd.

*Ruled

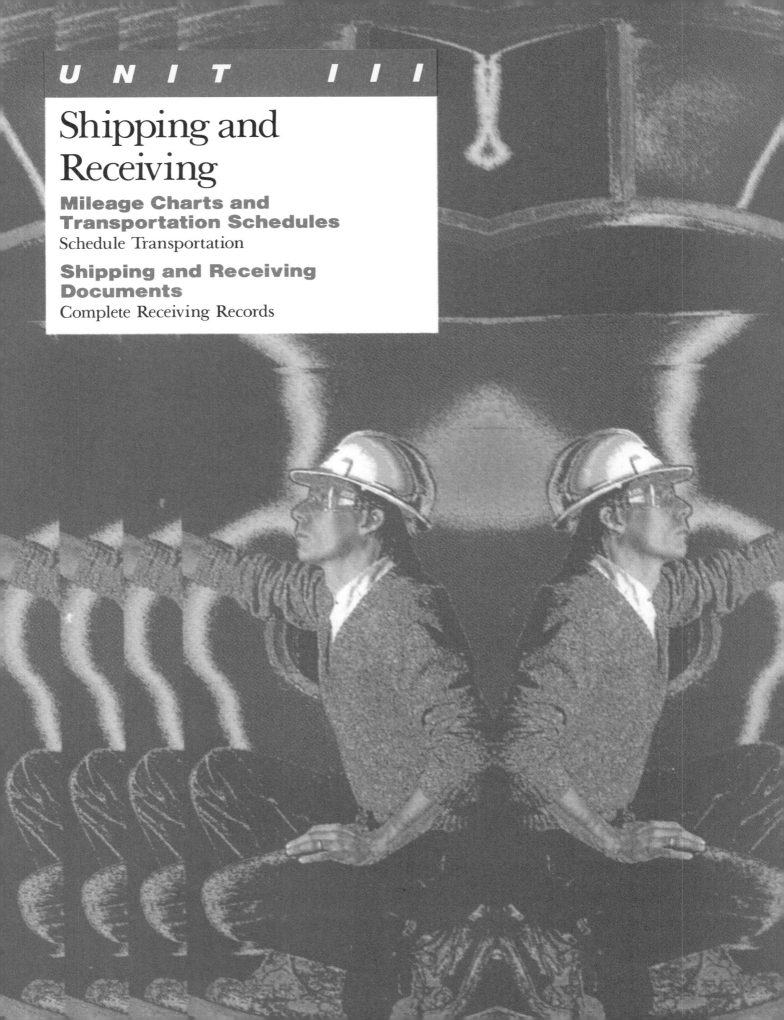

UNIT III

Shipping and Receiving

Mileage Charts and Transportation Schedules

Schedule Transportation

Shipping and Receiving Documents

Complete Receiving Records

MILEAGE CHARTS AND TRANSPORTATION SCHEDULES

If you work in the transportation industry, you depend on time and distance in many ways:

- *when* to go to work
- *when* to pick up people or things
- *when* to arrive at a place
- *when* to deliver people or things

To understand *when* in transporting people or things, you need to know

- starting point/arrival point
- how far? how fast?

SKILL PREVIEW

How do you use time and distance to schedule transportation? Show what you know about transportation terms. Find the defining word or phrase in Column B that best describes the transportation term in Column A. Write the letter in the blank provided.

Column A	Column B
_____ 1. mileage distance chart	a. where you are going to
_____ 2. origination point	b. instrument that measures distance traveled by a vehicle
_____ 3. destination point	c. measures distances on a map
_____ 4. odometer	d. where you start from
_____ 5. scale	e. measures miles automatically
_____ 6. transportation schedule	f. a plan that tells the amount of time you need to get to and from a destination point

UNDERSTANDING MILEAGE CHARTS AND TRANSPORTATION SCHEDULES

A **mileage distance chart** shows you how far it is from one city to another. The chart below shows the distance in miles between major cities and towns.

Suppose you want to find the distance between East St. Louis, Illinois, and Indianapolis, Indiana. Use a mileage distance chart like the one shown below.

First trace *down* the column that says East St. Louis. Then find the row that says Indianapolis, Indiana. Trace *across* that row and find the point where the two cities intersect, or meet. That number is the distance in miles between the two cities.

Note that on the mileage distance chart below, the distance between East St. Louis and Indianapolis is *240 miles.* It has been circled for you.

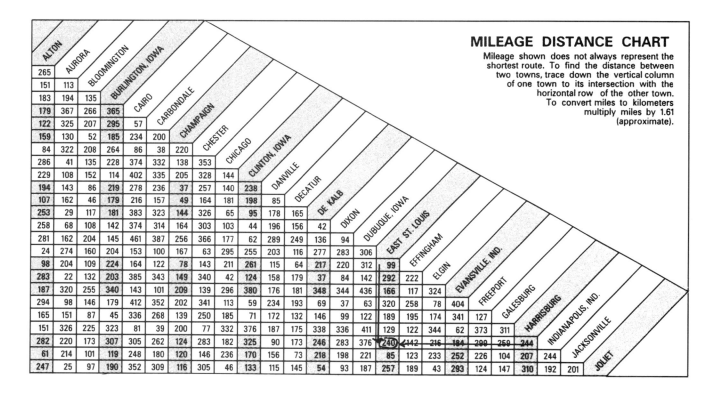

MILEAGE DISTANCE CHART

Mileage shown does not always represent the shortest route. To find the distance between two towns, trace down the vertical column of one town to its intersection with the horizontal row of the other town. To convert miles to kilometers multiply miles by 1.61 (approximate).

Use the mileage distance chart on page 72 to find the distance in miles between each of the cities given below.

1. The distance from Aurora, Illinois, to Cairo, Illinois, is ____ miles. (Aurora down, Cairo across)

2. The distance from Chester, Illinois, to DeKalb, Illinois, is ____ miles. (Chester down, DeKalb down and across)

3. The distance from Danville, Illinois, to Carbondale, Illinois, is ____ miles. (Danville down, Carbondale across)

4. The distance from Galesburg, Illinois, to Dixon, Illinois, is ____ miles. (Dixon down, Galesburg down and across)

You are correct if you wrote: 1. *367*; 2. *326*; 3. *236*; 4. *99*.

APPLIED PRACTICE 1: USING A MILEAGE DISTANCE CHART

Use the mileage distance chart on page 72 to find the distance between each city.

1. The distance from Burlington, Iowa, to Alton, Illinois, is ____ miles.

2. The distance from Decatur, Illinois, to Champaign, Illinois, is ____ miles.

3. The distance from Effingham, Illinois, to Chester, Illinois, is ____ miles.

4. The distance from Freeport, Illinois, to Chicago, Illinois, is ____ miles.

5. The distance from Dixon, Illinois, to Clinton, Iowa, is ____ miles.

6. The distance from Dubuque, Iowa, to Evansville, Indiana, is ____ miles.

7. The distance from Bloomington, Illinois, to Chicago, Illinois, is ____ miles.

8. The distance from Clinton, Iowa, to East St. Louis, Illinois, is ____ miles.

. . . .
Reading: Locating chart information at intersections of rows and columns

When you travel, you need to know *where* you will start, *when* you will leave, *how long* it will take you to get there, and *when* you will arrive. A bus schedule with starting points and destination points is shown below.

a	③ BUS LEAVES from Signal Plaza	④ Bus Arrives at Alexian Brothers	Does bus go on Signal Mtn. Rd. or US 27?	Does bus serve Provident Loop?	⑤ BUS ENDS at Broad St. & 12th St.	Bus goes on to serve Route:	Bus Arrives At CARTA Garage:
			WEEKDAYS				
A.M.	7:00	7:10	US 27	YES	7:40	#14	—
	8:20	8:35	Signal Mtn.	no	9:05	#28B	9:40
	8:40	b 8:50	Signal Mtn.	no	9:20	#14	—
	9:55	10:05	Signal Mtn.	no	10:30	—	c 10:40
P.M.	2:35	2:45	Signal Mtn.	no	3:15	#14	—
	3:55	4:15	Signal Mtn.	YES	4:50	#14	—
	5:20	5:30	Signal Mtn.	no	6:00	—	6:10

Scan the bus schedule to answer the following questions.

_____ 1. Locate the heading that reads Bus Leaves from Signal Plaza and write the letter that identifies it. (You were right if you found the heading in the first column at the top and wrote *a.*)

_____ 2. Locate the 8:50 A.M. arrival time and write the letter that identifies it. (If you found the time in the second column and went down to the middle of the row and wrote *b*, you were right.)

_____ 3. Write the time when the 9:55 A.M. bus arrives at the CARTA Garage and write the letter that identifies it. (You were right if you wrote *10:40 A.M., c.*)

Scan the bus schedule to answer the following questions.

1. Does the 2:35 P.M. bus that leaves from Signal Plaza go on Signal Mtn. Rd. or on US 27? _____

2. What time does the 5:20 P.M. bus from Signal Plaza arrive at Broad St. & 12th St.? _____

3. Does the 3:55 P.M. bus serve Provident Loop? _____

· · · · · · · · · · · ·
Reading: Reading two- or more column charts to obtain information

READING AN ODOMETER

Many jobs involve mileage that is not predictable and so can't be shown on a mileage chart. For example, pizza delivery persons do not know ahead of time how far away the customers live. So drivers use an **odometer** to determine mileage. An odometer is an instrument that measures distance traveled by a vehicle.

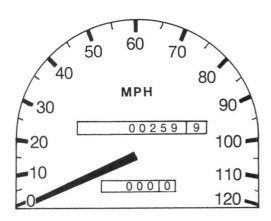

GUIDED PRACTICE

In the odometer shown above, the car's mileage is 259.9 miles. The number in the white box (9) shows the tenths of a mile. The number reads: two hundred fifty-nine and nine-tenths of a mile.

One pizza driver's odometer reads 13,220.8 at the beginning of the week. After the first day's deliveries, the odometer reads 13,263.3. To calculate mileage, subtract the starting odometer reading from the ending odometer reading.

Day 1	13,263.3	(ending odometer reading)
	−13,220.8	(starting odometer reading)
	42.5	(miles driven on day 1)

Calculate day 2's mileage. At the end of the day, the odometer reads 13,439.6.

Day 2	13,439.6	(ending odometer reading)
	−13,263.3	(starting odometer reading)
		(miles driven on day 2)

You are correct if you calculated: *176.3 miles* driven on day 2.

APPLIED PRACTICE 3: CALULATING MILEAGE

Calculate the driver's mileage for the whole week.

Day 3	**Day 4**	**Day 5**	**Week's Total Mileage**
			(Add 5 days' totals.)
13,485.8	13,522.3	13,584.3	
−13,439.6	−13,485.8	−13,522.3	
			_____

CALCULATING NUMBER OF MILES PER TANK

How far can you drive on a tank of gas? This is important to know for both your professional and personal life.

Step 1: Record your starting odometer reading.   23,992.6

Step 2: Record the odometer reading when you next fill your tank.   24,242.6

Step 3: Record the amount of fuel (in gallons) you filled your tank with.   10 gallons

Step 4: Calculate the mileage driven since you last filled the tank.

$$\begin{array}{r} 24{,}242.6 \\ -23{,}992.6 \\ \hline 250 \text{ miles} \end{array}$$

Step 5: Divide the number of miles driven by the number of gallons. $250 \div 10 = 25$ miles per gallon

Step 6: Multiply miles per gallon by the number of gallons the vehicle holds. $25 \times 15 = 375$ miles per tank

APPLIED PRACTICE 4: FIGURING MILEAGE

Follow the steps and use the information given to figure out the mileage per tank.

Step 1: 13,569.3

Step 2: 13,840.3

Step 3: 7 gallons

Step 4: Mileage = _____

Step 5: Miles per gallon = _____

Step 6: For 12-gallon tank = _____ miles per tank

MEASURING TIME AND RATE OF SPEED

A driver needs to know *how long* it will take to get from one city to another. Long-distance drivers are required to cover a specific distance in a certain amount of time. A driver also needs to know *how fast* to travel to cover a certain distance.

GUIDED PRACTICE

To find out *how long* a trip will take, divide the distance by an average rate of speed you will be driving.

Distance from Chicago to Milwaukee = 93 miles
Average rate of speed (miles per hour) = 55 mph
93 miles (distance) ÷ 55 (mph) = 1.69 hours

To find out *how fast* you must drive to cover a specific distance, divide the distance by the time.

To cover 1,200 miles in 20 hours, divide 1,200 by 20 = 60 mph.

APPLIED PRACTICE 5: CALCULATING TIME AND RATE OF SPEED

Calculate the time or rate of speed for each. Round your number to the nearest hundredth.

How long? (time)

1. 165 miles ÷ 55 mph = _____ hour(s)

2. 60 miles at 60 mph = _____ hour(s)

3. 260 miles at 65 mph = _____ hour(s)

How fast? (rate of speed)

4. 360 miles ÷ 6.5 hours = _____ mph

5. 800 miles in 14.5 hours = _____ mph

6. 585 miles in 9 hours = _____ mph

. . . .
Computation: Performing computations of addition, subtraction, multiplication, and division using whole numbers and decimals

DEVELOPING A LOCAL DELIVERY SCHEDULE

If you make local deliveries as a driver, you need to know the average number of stops you will make and the amount of time you will spend at each stop to figure out a delivery schedule.

Shown below is a portion of a shuttle bus schedule that shows times of pick-up and delivery from local hotels to the BWI Airport.

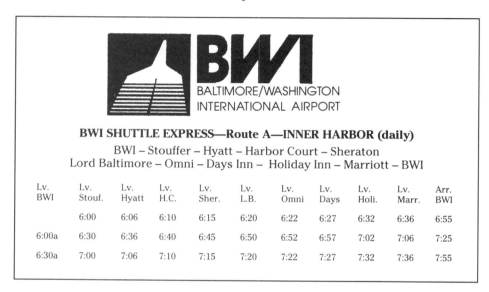

BWI BALTIMORE/WASHINGTON INTERNATIONAL AIRPORT

BWI SHUTTLE EXPRESS—Route A—INNER HARBOR (daily)

BWI – Stouffer – Hyatt – Harbor Court – Sheraton
Lord Baltimore – Omni – Days Inn – Holiday Inn – Marriott – BWI

Lv. BWI	Lv. Stouf.	Lv. Hyatt	Lv. H.C.	Lv. Sher.	Lv. L.B.	Lv. Omni	Lv. Days	Lv. Holi.	Lv. Marr.	Arr. BWI
	6:00	6:06	6:10	6:15	6:20	6:22	6:27	6:32	6:36	6:55
6:00a	6:30	6:36	6:40	6:45	6:50	6:52	6:57	7:02	7:06	7:25
6:30a	7:00	7:06	7:10	7:15	7:20	7:22	7:27	7:32	7:36	7:55

There are nine pick-up points on the first line of the schedule. They begin at the Stouffer Hotel at 6:00 A.M. and arrive at the BWI Airport at 6:55 A.M.

Use the first line of the schedule to answer the questions.

Example: What is the *longest* time between any of the stops? __6__ minutes

Subtract each Lv. (leave) time from the time to the right of it on the first line. (You are correct if you subtracted *6:55 – 6:36 = 19 minutes*).

1. What is the *shortest* time between stops? ____ minutes

2. If you are picked up at the Omni Hotel at 6:22 A.M. how long will it take you to arrive at the airport? ____ minutes

3. How many minutes does it take to drive from the Holiday Inn Hotel to the BWI Airport? ____ minutes

You are correct if you answered: 1. *2 minutes*; 2. *33 minutes*; 3. *23 minutes*.

Local delivery schedules must account for

- number of stops
- average time per stop
- distance from one stop to the next

For local deliveries you need to **estimate**, or guess, how long it will take to drive from one place to the next. Driving 5 miles on a highway at 60 mph might take 5 minutes. But in local traffic, driving 5 miles might take 15 to 20 minutes.

Given the information below, complete the delivery schedule. The driver is leaving the warehouse at 7:45 A.M. and wants to make the last delivery by 10:30 A.M. (Add the time between stops in column 1 to the delivery time in column 2).

Driving Time + Time per Stop   **Delivery Schedule**

7:45 A.M. (leave warehouse)

1. 18 minutes   +   7:45 A.M. = 8:03 A.M.

2. 19 minutes   +   8:03 A.M. = _____ A.M.

3. 16 minutes   +   _____ = _____ A.M.

4. 33 minutes   +   _____ = _____ A.M.

5. 20 minutes   +   _____ = _____ A.M.

6. 27 minutes   +   _____ = _____ A.M.

WORKWISE

Think about all the functions you perform on a typical day at your workplace. List six to eight activities that you do on a routine basis. Estimate how long it takes you to do each job. Begin with a starting time for the first job. Then keep adding on the minutes it takes to complete each function. When you are finished, you will have completed a time schedule similar to the ones made out by drivers who make local deliveries.

. . . .
Reading: Reading two- or more column charts to obtain information
Computation: Planning and scheduling time

SCHEDULE TRANSPORTATION

	Bus leaves CARTA Garage At:	**1** BUS STARTS at 12th Street & Broad Street	Does bus go on Market or 5th to US 27?	**2** Bus Arrives at Palisades & Signal Mtn. Blvd.	**3** BUS ARRIVES at Signal Plaza
			WEEKDAYS		
A.M.	6:20	6:30	Market	6:55	7:00
	—	7:40	Market	8:15	8:20
	—	8:08	Market	8:35	8:40
	—	9:20	Market	9:50	9:55
P.M.	1:50	2:00	Market	2:30	2:35
	—	3:15	Market	3:50	3:55
	—	4:50	5th to US 27	5:15	5:20

Scan the bus schedule to answer the following questions.

1. At what time does the afternoon bus leave the CARTA Garage? _____

2. Where does the 9:20 A.M. bus arrive at 9:50 A.M.?

   _____

3. Does the bus that leaves the CARTA Garage at 1:50 P.M. go on Market or on 5th to U.S. 27? _____

4. Is the schedule a weekday, holiday, or weekend schedule? _____

5. How many minutes does it take the 8:15 A.M. bus at Palisades and Signal Mtn. Blvd. to arrive at Signal Plaza? _____

6. At what time does the 4:50 P.M. bus from 12th Street and Broad Street arrive at Signal Plaza? _____

7. When does the bus that arrives at Palisades and Signal Mtn. Blvd. at 3:50 P.M. arrive at Signal Plaza? _____

8. How long does it take the 6:20 A.M. bus to arrive at Signal Plaza? _____

SHIPPING AND RECEIVING DOCUMENTS

A purchase is shipped to your workplace, and someone receives it. **Shipping and receiving documents** must be processed to prove that the purchase was completed. **Shipping and receiving clerks** find the most cost-effective ways to have purchases shipped from the **vendor**, or seller.

SKILL PREVIEW

You work for Pro Racing Distributors. You receive a shipment from Carter Express. The delivery person unloads 11 boxes onto the dock and asks you to "sign off" on the **freight bill**. You count 11 boxes received. Two of the boxes are damaged.

As a receiving clerk, you have a copy of the original **purchase order**. You check that against the freight bill given to you by the delivery person. **Your order reads:**

NO. PACKAGES	DESCRIPTION OF ARTICLES, SPECIAL MARKS AND EXCEPTIONS	* WEIGHT (Subject to Correction)	CLASS or RATE	CHECK COLUMN
12	Boxes Gloves #HT8	562	F.C. 220	

The freight bill reads:

NO. PCS.	DESCRIPTION	WEIGHT	RATE	PAYMENT TERMS Prepaid ☐ Collect ☒
12	Boxes Gloves #HT8	562	F.C. 220	$220.00

You count the shipment again, finding 11 boxes. Two of the boxes are damaged. The receiving portion of the freight bill is shown below. After the words *received in good condition except as noted,* write the number of boxes you received and the number of boxes that were damaged. On the second line, write the name of your firm (company you work for). Finally, write your name. (See the full documents on pages 163, 165 and 167.)

RECEIVED IN GOOD CONDITION EXCEPT AS NOTED:
FIRM _____
BY _____
I.C.C. REGULATIONS REQUIRE PAYMENT WITHIN 15 DAYS

LOCATING SHIPPING INFORMATION

As a shipping and receiving clerk, you need to know how to have an order shipped to your company.

You can find shipping and delivery companies in the **yellow pages** of a telephone directory. Before you call to compare which company will provide the best service, you need to have the following information on hand:

- **weight** of the package or shipment
- **dimensions** (size)
- **declared value** (what the shipment is worth)
- **destination** (full address of place shipment is going to: street name and number, city, state, zip code)
- **who is paying** for shipping: **shipper** (sender), or **consignee** (receiver)

Ground and air delivery services generally offer the following types of services:

- international delivery (to other countries)
- second day (priority) delivery (by second business day)
- next day delivery or overnight/express delivery
- Saturday delivery

GUIDED PRACTICE

You can use trucking companies (motor freight) for large shipments. *Partial* and *full load* shipments are both available. Depending on how many packages are being sent, you may need only part of a truck. Some trucking companies have restrictions on where they can **cart**, or carry, shipments.

```
┌─────────────────────────────────────────────┐
│   ( Trucking-Motor Freight )                  │
│                                               │
│  ABF FREIGHT SYSTEM INC                       │
│     1260 Terminal Rd --------------------788-1591 │
│  ANR FREIGHT SYSTEM INC                       │
│     1101 Harding Ct Indianapolis ---------788-4766 │
│  ACTION TRANSPORTING SERVICE                  │
│     2444 S West ------------------------788-9953 │
└─────────────────────────────────────────────┘
```

1. In the yellow pages, motor freight is also listed as _____.

2. Look at the yellow pages entry above. You can call ABF Freight at _____.

When you are making decisions about shipping, you should compare motor freight and air freight:

- Motor freight is generally less expensive.
- Air freight is faster.

```
Air—(Cont'd)
   Conditioning-Room Units See
      Air Conditioning Equipment-Room
         Units ---------------------------26
   Conditioning Supplies & Parts -------26
   Conditioning Systems-Cleaning-----26
   Courier Service -----------------------26
   Craft Dealers See
      Aircraft Dealers --------------------29
   Curtains & Screens---------------------26
   Cylinders See
      Cylinders-Air & Hydraulic --------442
      Valves ------------------------------1460
   Duct Cleaning See
      Ventilating Systems-Cleaning-1464
   Express Service See
      Air Cargo & Package Express
         Service-----------------------14
      Air Courier Service-----------------26
```

┌─────────────────────────────────────┐
│ **Air Cargo & Package**   │
│ **Express Service**   │
└─────────────────────────────────────┘

A M TRANSPORT
  Pick Up ★ 9 AM Delivery
  Same Day Or Overnight Delivery
  Weekend & Holiday Service
  999 W Troy Av --------------------788-4140
ADCOM EXPRESS
  See Ad Under Air Cargo & Package Express
  Service-Business To Business Directory
  3322½ W 10 ----------------------**634-0063**
AIR EXPRESS INTERNATIONAL CORP
  1936 S Lynhurst Suite P -------------243-3231
AIR FREIGHT FORWARDING CO
  5744 W 71st -----------------------291-3956

3. Look at the yellow pages entries above. Air Freight is listed under the heading *Air Cargo and* _____.

4. A M Transport offers 9:00 A.M. delivery, same day or _____ delivery, and weekend and _____ service.

You are correct if you answered: 1. *trucking*; 2. *788-1591*; 3. *Package Express Service*; 4. *overnight, holiday*.

APPLIED PRACTICE 1: LOCATING INFORMATION

Check page 82 for the five pieces of information you need to have on hand before you call a shipping company. List them here.

1. _____

2. _____

3. _____

4. _____

5. _____

. . . .
Reading: Identifying factual details and specifications within text

COMPARING PARCEL DELIVERY SERVICES

Both private companies and the U.S. Postal Service offer **parcel services**. Private parcel companies offer timely delivery for smaller shipments at a competitive cost. They use both air and ground routes for business and home delivery. Parcel services are listed in the yellow pages under *Delivery Service.*

The U.S. Postal Service offers parcel, postal, and air mail services. This agency is listed in your local telephone directory under the heading *Government.*

GUIDED PRACTICE

Look at these yellow pages entries for private parcel companies. Then answer the questions that follow.

1. Does DHL Worldwide Express deliver internationally? _____

2. How many days does this delivery take? _____

Now look at the telephone numbers listed for the U.S. Postal Service.

Postal Inquiry Claims and Rates	464-6000
Zip Code Information 8:00 AM - 4:30 PM	464-6150
Passport Information	464-6378
EXPRESS MAIL - Mon - Fri. 8 AM - 5 PM	464-6273
After 5 PM, Sat., Sun. & Holidays	464-6253
Air Mail Facility Open 24 Hours	464-6251

3. What number could you call for Express Mail information on weekdays during business hours?

   _____

4. For Express Mail service during evenings, weekends, and holidays, call

   _____ .

You are correct if you answered: 1. *yes*; 2. *1 to 3 days*; 3. *464-6273*; 4. *464-6253.*

Look at the yellow pages entries below. Then answer the questions that follow.

EMERY & PUROLATOR	TWA AIR CARGO
• Any size, any weight, anywhere • Worldwide air express service • Next morning throughout USA • Door to door **EMERY & Purolator**	• Air Freight • Priority Air Express • NFO Small Package Express Service • TRAC Computer Tracing **TWA**
PICK UP & INFORMATION EMERY & PUROLATOR WORLDWIDE COURIER & CARGO Toll Free-Dial "1" & Then --- 800 443-6379	*AIR CARGO* TRANS WORLD AIRLINES INC International Airport ------------248-3673 *SMALL PACKAGE EXPRESS SERVICE* TRANS WORLD AIRLINES INC Toll Free-Dial "1" & Then --- 800 638-7380

1. Which delivery service ships any size, any weight, anywhere?

   _____

2. Which delivery service offers small package express service?

   _____

3. Which delivery service offers worldwide air express service?

   _____

WORKWISE

Use your telephone directory to call a delivery service. Ask what types of service it provides and list them in the space provided below.

1. Company name _____

2. Services

   a. _____

   b. _____

   c. _____

. . . .
Reading: Identifying factual details and specifications within text; Selecting parts of text or visual materials to complete a task

INTERPRETING SHIPPING DOCUMENTS

Once you have decided how to make your shipment, documentation must follow. **Documents** are official papers, forms, or records that prove that something occurred.

One document you must fill out is a **shipping label** from the company that you have chosen. The shipping label will include delivery instructions and the **declared value** (cost of replacement) of the contents of the package.

Another document you will get is a **bill of lading**, or packing slip, that comes with the shipment. Both documents usually include the declared value and the class of the shipment. The actual price or cost of the shipment might not be included.

GUIDED PRACTICE

You are a shipping clerk for Worth Corporation. You are sending a delivery to a customer. Use the following bill of lading to identify shipping information.

Consigned to.... *SPEED RACER APPAREL*
Destination.... *123 Racine Blvd., Detroit* ....State of.. *Michigan* ....County of.. *Jackson*
Route.... *Dock #3*
Delivering Carrier.. *Carter Express, 6015 Pendleton Ave.* .... *Anderson, IN* *46013*

NO. PACKAGES	DESCRIPTION OF ARTICLES, SPECIAL MARKS AND EXCEPTIONS	*WEIGHT (Subject to Correction)	CLASS or RATE	CHECK COLUMN	Signature of Consignor.
40	*Boxes Driver's Suits* *#D24*	*805*	*FC300*		If charges are to be prepaid, write or stamp here, "To be Prepaid."
					Received $_____ to apply in prepayment of the charges on the property described hereon.

* If the shipment moves between two ports by a carrier by water, the law requires that the bill of lading shall state whether it is "carrier's or shipper's weight."
Note.—Where the rate is dependent on value, shippers are required to state specifically in writing the agreed or declared value of the property.
The agreed or declared value of the property is hereby specifically stated by the shipper to be not exceeding $............per............ Agent or Cashier.

Worth Corporation ....Shipper, Per *K. Robbins* AGENT *Carter Express* PER............ ①
Permanent postoffice address of shipper.. *301 N. Harrison, Alexandria, IN 46001*

1. Look at the two lines at the bottom of the bill. Who is the shipment *from* (shipper) ?_____

2. Look at the first line of the bill. Who is the shipment being **consigned** (sent) **to**?

   _____

3. Is the shipment **prepaid** (by the shipper) or **C.O.D.** (cash on delivery) by the consignor? _____

4. What is the **route** (place of delivery)? _____

5. How many *packages* are being shipped? _____

You are correct if you answered: 1. *Worth Corporation*; 2. *Speed Racer Apparel*; 3. *C.O.D.*; 4. *Dock #3*; 5. *40*.

You are a Worth Corporation shipping clerk preparing a bill of lading. Use the following shipping information to fill in the appropriate numbered blanks on the bill of lading.

- The shipper's number is 9051.
- The shipment is to be picked up at 10:00 a.m. on April 9, 1993 from the Worth Corporation.
- The shipment is to be consigned (sent) to Pro Racing Distributors.
- The destination (address) is 1779 Winding Way, Daytona, Florida, Orange County.
- Route instructions should be picked up at the south entrance of the shipping bay.
- The carrier is Carter Express, at 6015 Pendleton Ave., Anderson, IN 46013.
- You are shipping 12 boxes of gloves, item #HT8, that weigh 562 lb, class FC220.

Uniform Domestic Straight Bill of Lading, adopted by Carriers in Official, Southern, Western and Illinois Classification Territories, March 15, 1922, as amended August 1, 1930 and June 15, 1941

UNIFORM STRAIGHT BILL OF LADING
ORIGINAL—NOT NEGOTIABLE.

Shipper's No.......................................

Company   Agent's No. ....

RECEIVED, subject to the classifications and tariffs in effect on the date of the issue of this Bill of Lading.

At .... **19** ...... **From** ....

the property described below, in apparent good order, except as noted (contents and condition of contents of packages unknown), marked, consigned, and destined as indicated below, which said company (the word company being understood throughout this contract as meaning any person or corporation in possession of the property under the contract) agrees to carry to its usual place of delivery at said destination, if on its own road or its own water line, otherwise to deliver to another carrier on the route to said destination. It is mutually agreed, as to each carrier of all or any of said property over all or any portion of said route to destination, and as to each party at any time interested in all or any of said property, that every service to be performed hereunder shall be subject to all the conditions not prohibited by law, whether printed or written, herein contained, including the conditions on back hereof, which are hereby agreed to by the shipper and accepted for himself and his assigns.

(Mail or street address of consignee—For purposes of notification only)

Consigned to...

Destination.. State of.................................... County of..

Route...

Delivering Carrier... Car Initial.. Car No.....................

NO. PACKAGES	DESCRIPTION OF ARTICLES, SPECIAL MARKS AND EXCEPTIONS	* WEIGHT (Subject to Correction)	CLASS or RATE	CHECK COLUMN	Subject to Section 7 of conditions, if this shipment is to be delivered to the consignee without recourse on the consignor, the consignor shall sign the following statement: The carrier shall not make delivery of this shipment without payment of freight and all other lawful charges.
					Signature of Consignor.
					If charges are to be prepaid, write or stamp here, "To be Prepaid."
					Received $............................ to apply in prepayment of the charges on the property described hereon.
					Agent or Cashier.
					Per............................ (The signature here acknowledges only the amount prepaid.)
					Charges Advanced:

* If the shipment moves between two ports by a carrier by water, the law requires that the bill of lading shall state whether it is "carrier's or shipper's weight."
Note.—Where the rate is dependent on value, shippers are required to state specifically in writing the agreed or declared value of the property.
The agreed or declared value of the property is hereby specifically stated by the shipper to be not exceeding $........................per........................

....Shipper, Per........................   AGENT........................   PER........................ ①

Permanent postoffice address of shipper..

The Fibre Boxes used for this shipment conform to the specifications set forth in the box maker's certificate thereon and all other requirements of Rule 41 of the Consolidated Freight Classification.

Reading: Identifying factual details and specifications within text; **Writing:** Entering appropriate information onto a form

PROCESSING DOCUMENTS OF RECEIPT

Two documents shipping and receiving clerks may use are

- **bill of lading** (a slip that comes with a shipment)
- **receiving record** (a form you fill out when you get the shipment)

GUIDED PRACTICE

You are the receiving clerk for Pro Racing. Before signing off on the Worth Corporation shipment, follow these steps:

1. *Count* the **quantity**, or number, of packages (30 boxes total, 3 boxes damaged).

2. *Compare the count* you have with the number that should have been delivered, according to the receiving record.

Fill out the bill of lading as follows:

1. Find the column labeled **No. Packages**. On the blank line, write the total number of boxes you ordered that should have been shipped to you.

2. Put a check mark (✔) in the **Check Column**.

NO. PACKAGES	DESCRIPTION OF ARTICLES, SPECIAL MARKS AND EXCEPTIONS	* WEIGHT (Subject to Correction)	CLASS or RATE	CHECK COLUMN
10	Helmet Slips #H39	80	FC 40	
20	Material #FR14	360	FC 150	

3. On the receiving record, write the number of boxes that were damaged.

4. Write the name of your firm.

5. Write your name.

```
RECEIVED IN GOOD CONDITION EXCEPT AS NOTED:

FIRM _____

BY _____
        I.C.C. REGULATIONS REQUIRE PAYMENT WITHIN 15 DAYS
```

You are correct if you wrote: 1. *30*; 2. *check mark (✔) in the check column*; 3. *3 boxes damaged*; 4. *Pro Racing*; 5. *your name*.

. . . .

Reading: Reading two- or more column charts to obtain information
Writing: Entering appropriate information onto a form

Complete the receiving record for the 30 boxes you received from Worth Corporation with the following information:

1. The receipt number is 79061.

2. Write today's date.

3. After *received from*, write the name of the shipper.

4. After *by*, write your name.

5. and 6. Check the information on the bill of lading on page 88 to fill out the quantity of helmet slips you received and the identification number (#) of the articles.

Receipt No. _____	_____ 19 _____

RECEIVED FROM _____

By _____

_____

REQUISITION NO.

_____

In good order the following:

QUANTITY	NO.	DESCRIPTION OF PACKAGES

TOPS FORM 3014
LITHO IN U. S. A.
ORIGINAL

Sign here _____

• • • • • • • • • • • •

Reading: Reading two- or more column charts to obtain information
Writing: Entering appropriate information onto a form

USING POSTAL RATE TABLES

Postage **rates** usually depend on two things: the weight of a package, and the **zone** (the area to which the package is being shipped). The heavier the package and the farther it is sent, the more it costs to ship it.

Several of the larger parcel delivery companies, such as United Parcel Service and Federal Express, have computers that will calculate postage rates based on weight, zone, and the requested speed of delivery. If your company does not have such a computer, you'll need to use a **postal rate table** to find the cost of shipping.

GUIDED PRACTICE

Each local post office has a zone chart based on the first three digits of a zip code (called the **prefix**). What is the prefix of this zip code: 32503? _____ (If you wrote *325*, you are correct.)

Now practice reading the zone chart. Write the correct zone for each prefix.

Prefix	Zone
Example: 386-394	4
1. 395	_____
2. 407-409	_____
3. 410	_____
4. 460-462	_____

```
-----------------------------------
ZIP CODE
PREFIXES                        ZONE
-----------------------------------
386-394.................................4
395.......................................5
396-399.................................4
400-406.................................2
407-409.................................3
410.......................................2
411-422.................................3
423-424.................................2
425-426.................................3
427-432.................................2
433-449.................................3
450-455.................................2
456-457.................................3
458-459.................................2
460-462.................................1
```

You are correct if you answered: 1. *5*; 2. *3*; 3. *2*; 4. *1.*

WORKWISE

Go to your local post office and ask how much it would cost you to send a package. Take a package for the mail clerk to weigh and have the zip code of the package destination. Rate for sending package: _____

The postal rate chart below shows the rate (cost) of shipping based on both weight and zone. To find the rate of a package, you need to

- locate the *weight* (on the left side of the chart)
- follow the row across (from left to right) to the *zone*

Weight, up to but not exceeding— pound(s)	Local 1, 2, and 3	ZONES 4	5	6	7	8
	PRIORITY MAIL*					
1	2.90	2.90	2.90	2.90	2.90	2.90
2	2.90	2.90	2.90	2.90	2.90	2.90
3	4.10	4.10	4.10	4.10	4.10	4.10
4	4.65	4.65	4.65	4.65	4.65	4.65
5	5.45	5.45	5.45	5.45	5.45	5.45
6	5.55	5.75	6.10	6.85	7.65	8.60
7	5.70	6.10	6.70	7.55	8.50	9.65
8	5.90	6.50	7.30	8.30	9.40	10.70
9	6.10	7.00	7.95	9.05	10.25	11.75
10	6.35	7.55	8.55	9.80	11.15	12.80
11	6.75	8.05	9.20	10.55	12.05	13.80
12	7.15	8.55	9.80	11.30	12.90	14.85
13	7.50	9.10	10.40	12.05	13.80	15.90
14	7.90	9.60	11.05	12.80	14.65	16.95
15	8.30	10.10	11.65	13.55	15.55	18.00

Find the rates for the following packages:

	weight	zone	rate
1.	2 lb.	4	_____
2.	6 lb.	7	_____
3.	15 lb.	3	_____
4.	5 lb.	5	_____

You are shipping a 9-pound and a 3-pound package to zip code 39605.

Use the zone chart on page 90 and the postal rate chart above to answer the questions that follow.

5. To what zone is the package being shipped? _____

6. What is the rate for the 9-pound package? _____

7. What is the rate for the 3-pound package? _____

. . . .
Reading: Reading two- or more column charts to obtain information

COMPLETE RECEIVING RECORDS

Look at the bill of lading below. Some information has been filled in for you. You will find a complete bill of lading on page 163.

The Fibre Boxes used for this shipment conform to the specifications set forth in the box maker's certificate thereon and all other requirements of Rule 41 of the Consolidated Freight Classification.

Uniform Domestic Straight Bill of Lading, adopted by Carriers in Official, Southern, Western and Illinois Classification Territories, March 15, 1922, as amended August 1, 1930 and June 15, 1941

UNIFORM STRAIGHT BILL OF LADING
ORIGINAL—NOT NEGOTIABLE.

Shipper's No. ....
Company   Agent's No. ....

RECEIVED, subject to the classifications and tariffs in effect on the date of the issue of this Bill of Lading.

At _____ **19** ____ **From** _____

the property described below, in apparent good order, except as noted (contents and condition of contents of packages unknown), marked, consigned, and destined as indicated below, which said company (the word company being understood throughout this contract as meaning any person or corporation in possession of the property under the contract) agrees to carry to its usual place of delivery at said destination, if on its own road or its own water line, otherwise to deliver to another carrier on the route to said destination. It is mutually agreed, as to each carrier of all or any of said property over all or any portion of said route to destination, and as to each party at any time interested in all or any of said property, that every service to be performed hereunder shall be subject to all the conditions not prohibited by law, whether printed or written, herein contained, including the conditions on back hereof, which are hereby agreed to by the shipper and accepted for himself and his assigns.

(Mail or street address of consignee—For purposes of notification only)

Consigned to _Transit Towers, Inc._
Destination _1070 State Road 37W, Cuba_   State of _Kansas_   County of _____
Route _drop bay 10_
Delivering Carrier _Clipper Express   2462 S. West   Indianapolis IN 46240_

NO. PACKAGES	DESCRIPTION OF ARTICLES, SPECIAL MARKS AND EXCEPTIONS	* WEIGHT (Subject to Correction)	CLASS or RATE	CHECK COLUMN	Subject to Section 7 of conditions, if this shipment is to be delivered to the consignee without recourse on the consignor, the consignor shall sign the following statement:
100	_Skids of copper coil #8_	_2,600_	_F.C.500_		The carrier shall not make delivery of this shipment without payment of freight and all other lawful charges.
					_____ Signature of Consignor

* If the shipment moves between two ports by a carrier by water, the law requires that the bill of lading shall state whether it is "carrier's or shipper's weight."
Note.—Where the rate is dependent on value, shippers are required to state specifically in writing the agreed or declared value of the property.
The agreed or declared value of the property is hereby specifically stated by the shipper to be not exceeding $ _____ per _____

If charges are to be prepaid, write or stamp here, "To be Prepaid."

Angus Metals Inc. _____ Shipper, Per _N. Angus_   AGENT _Clipper Express_ PER _T. Janus_ ①
Permanent postoffice address of shipper _Angus Metals, 1302 Pipe Creek Rd., Fairmont, TX 7072_

Use the information below to complete the receiving record on page 167.

1. The receipt number is 50878.

2. Write today's date.

3. You received the shipment from Angus Metals.

4. The requisition number is 4594.

5. You received 100 skids of #8 copper coil.

6. Three skids are damaged.

7. Sign your name at the bottom of the form.

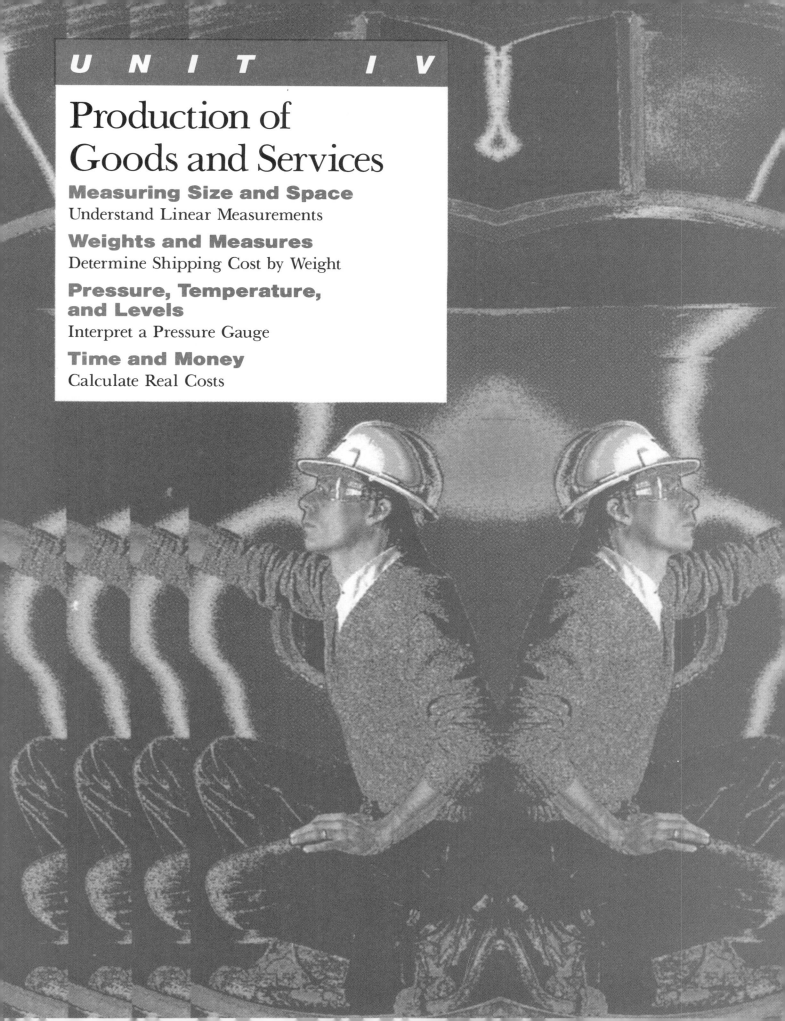

UNIT IV

MEASURING SIZE AND SPACE

Have you ever gone to buy paint or carpet for a room? How did you know how much paint or carpet to buy? You may have estimated the floor space to know how much carpet to buy. You may have measured the wall space to know how much paint to buy. If you did, you were able to buy enough carpet or paint for the room. Knowing how to measure an area is a useful skill both at home and at work.

SKILL PREVIEW

You work for Pools & More, Inc. Your company sells, installs, fixes, and repaints pools of all shapes and sizes. Shown below are drawings of two pools your company sells. Use the drawings to answer the questions that follow.

Olympic Pool   **Collegiate Pool**

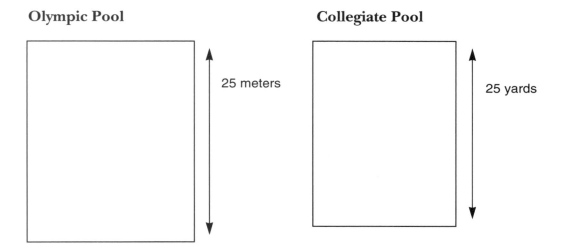

25 meters   25 yards

1. What measuring tool could you use to find the length of the pools? _____

2. What is the length of the olympic pool? _____

3. What is the length of the collegiate pool? _____

4. Which pool is longer? _____

UNDERSTANDING UNITS OF MEASUREMENT

In this lesson, you will be working with

- **linear measurement**—one dimension (for example, length *or* width)
- **surface area**—two dimensions (length *and* width)

If you are a construction worker, you might say, "That porch wall is 10 feet high." The **linear measurement unit** you are using is *feet*. If you are a farmer you might say, "That field plot is 1 square mile." The **surface measurement unit** is *miles*. If you are a cement mixer, you might say, "That sidewalk will be 30 cubic feet of cement." The measurement unit is *cubic feet*.

These are the linear measuring tools you might use at work:

- **ruler**— to measure under 12 inches or about 30 centimeters
- **measuring tape** or **steel tape**—to measure from 3 to 500 feet
- **yard stick** or **meter stick**—to measure under a yard or meter

In the United States, we use two types of measurement units. Review the **English** (or **U.S. customary**) **system** and **metric system** below. Study the relationship between the two systems.

English (U.S. customary)	Metric
25.4 millimeters (mm) 1 inch = 2.54 centimeters (cm)	1 millimeter (mm) = .03937 in.
1 foot (ft.) = 12 in. = 30.48 cm .3048 meters (m)	1 centimeter (cm) = .3937 in.
1 yard (yd.) = 3 ft. = .9144 m	1 meter (m) = 3.2808 ft. 1.0936 yd.
1 mile (mi.) = 1,760 yd. = 1,609.3 m 5,280 ft. = 1.6093 kilometers (km)	1 kilometer (km) = 1,093.6 yd. .6217 mi.

English/Metric Ruler

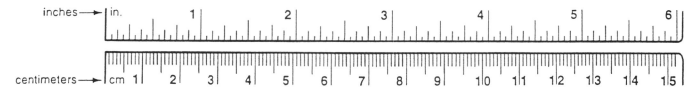

Use the ruler and information on page 96 to circle which word is correct.

1. An inch is longer/shorter than a centimeter.
      (choose one)

2. A yard is longer/shorter than a meter.
      (choose one)

3. A mile is longer/shorter than a kilometer.
      (choose one)

You are correct if you circled: 1. *longer*; 2. *shorter*; 3. *longer*.

APPLIED PRACTICE 1: UNDERSTANDING UNITS OF MEASUREMENT

Which *measurement tool* would you use to measure the items below? Which *units of measurement* would you work with? Use the information on page 96 to choose and circle the correct answers.

1. To buy the correct size screw   mm/m

2. To measure the distance   yd./mi.

3. To replace a kitchen counter   cm/m   ruler/meter stick

4. To replace a ceiling tile   in./mi.   ruler/tape measure

APPLIED PRACTICE 2: CHOOSING UNITS OF MEASUREMENT

Which measurement units would most likely be used to measure each of the following? Use abbreviations of U.S. customary and metric units. More than one answer is correct.

1. nail length _____

2. telephone cord length _____

3. fence post height _____

4. bolt width _____

5. floor width _____

. . . .
Computation: Performing basic measurement tasks including the use of conversion tables
Problem Solving: Comparing and contrasting

UNDERSTANDING INCREMENTS OF MEASUREMENT

The lines on rulers, tapes measures, and yard sticks or meter sticks are called **increments.** Each increment represents a number. That number is the **measurement** of whatever it is you are measuring.

On your job, you use both **exact** and **estimated** measurements. An estimated measurement is a guess. When measuring *exactly*, check your measurement at least twice. When *estimating* measurements:

- **Round down** if the number is less than half of the increment or number (for example, round $3\frac{5}{16}$" to 3").
- **Round up** if the number is half or more of the increment or number (for example, round $2\frac{7}{8}$" to the nearest inch up, to 3").

GUIDED PRACTICE

This is an English system ruler. Read the rulers to answer the questions.

Bar A

1. How many increments are there in an inch (including the 1-inch line)? ____ (You are correct if you answered *16.*)

2. Look at bar A. How many lines are there up to and including the line at the end of bar A? ____ (If you answered *7, which is $\frac{7}{16}$"*, you were right.)

Find the correct length for each section of ruler shown below. The length is shaded. Then reduce your answer to the lowest terms.

Example: $\frac{8}{16} = \frac{4}{8} = \frac{2}{4} = \frac{1}{2}$

3.

____ inch

4.
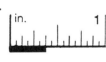
____ inch

5.

____ inch

6.

____ inch

You are correct if you wrote: 3. $\frac{15}{16}$; 4. $\frac{6}{16}$ or $\frac{3}{8}$; 5. $\frac{4}{16}$ or $\frac{1}{4}$; 6. $\frac{12}{16}$ or $\frac{3}{4}$.

Using an English system ruler, find the exact measurement of the washer (in diameter) and screw shown below.

1. ____

2. ____

Estimate the length of the object to the nearest increment.

3.

    a. What is the length of the tubing to the nearest inch? ____

    b. What is the length of the tubing to the nearest $\frac{1}{4}$"? ____

4.

    a. What is the length of the nail to the nearest $\frac{1}{2}$"? ____

    b. What is the length of the nail to the nearest inch? ____

5.

    a. What is the length of the bolt to the nearest $\frac{1}{8}$" ? ____

    b. What is the length of the bolt to the nearest $\frac{1}{4}$"? ____

SELF-CHECK

Did you reduce your answers to the lowest terms possible? Did you double check your measurements? If you are not sure about reducing numbers to lowest terms, check with your instructor.

Computation: Performing basic measurement tasks determining length; Reading and interpreting basic measurement and numerical readings on measurement instruments

CONVERTING UNITS OF MEASURE

If you measured the length of a countertop at 10 feet, but the materials you need are sold by the yard, what would you do?

Just as you can't add 3 apples to 3 oranges and get 6 apples, you can't add 3 feet to 3 yards and get 6 feet. By following the process below, you can **convert**, or change, the measurements to the same unit.

Before you add, subtract, multiply, or divide measurements, the **measurement units** must be the same.

GUIDED PRACTICE

You own a paint and wallpapering business. You have been hired to install a border in the Murillos' new family room.

English (U.S. customary)	
1 inch (in.)	1 foot (ft.) = 12 in.
1 yard (yd.) = 3 ft.	1 mile (mi.) = 1,760 yd. = 5,280 ft.

You have measured the Murillos' family room. You need at least 35 feet of the wallpaper border. You generally buy 5 extra feet to allow for any problems. So, you need approximately 40 feet. The Murillos' have chosen a border that is measured in 5-yard rolls.

How will you convert 40 feet into yards? You know that there are 3 feet in a yard. You need to divide 40 by 3. Round your answer to the nearest yard. $40 \div 3 = 13.3$ (rounded off to 13 yd.)

1. You can buy only complete rolls. How many 5-yard rolls do you need to buy?
   13 yd. ÷ 5 yd. rolls = _____ , rounded off to _____ rolls

You're correct if you answered: 1. *2.6, 3.*

Practice converting the following measurements. Round your answers to the nearest whole number (for example, round 1.4 yd. to 1 yd., 280.79 mi. to 281 mi.). Don't forget the units.

2. 350 ft. to yd.
   $350 \div 3 =$ _____ yds.

3. 70 in. to ft.
   $70 \div 12 =$ _____ ft.

4. 3 mi. to ft.
   $3 \times 5,280 =$ _____ ft.

You're correct if you answered: 2. *117*; 3. *6*; 4. *15,840.*

You are an order clerk for Grant's Block, Brick & Stone Company. These are some conversions you might need to make as part of your job.

Conversions

Ton
1 short ton = 20 short hundredweight (cwt.) = 2,000 pounds (lb.)
1 long ton = 20 long cwt. = 2,240 lb.

Hundredweight (cwt.)
1 short cwt. = .05 short tons = 100 lb.
1 long cwt. = .05 long tons = 112 lb.

Hal Jenkins has ordered 50 long hundredweight of cinder blocks and 400 pounds of limestone gravel.

Step 1: Use the chart above to convert Hal's order.

1. Cinder blocks cost $100 per long ton. Convert 50 long hundredweight to long tons. Then multiply that amount × $100 to figure out the cost.
   1 long hundredweight (cwt.) = .05 long tons
   50 long cwt. × .05 long tons = _____ long tons
   $100 × _____ long tons = _____ dollars

2. Limestone costs $26 per short hundredweight. Convert 400 lb. to short hundredweight. Then multiply that amount × $26 to figure out the cost.
   1 short cwt. = 100 lb. So, _____ short cwt. = 400 lb.
   _____ × $26 = _____

Step 2: Fill in the order form below. Compute the total cost.

Grant's Block, Brick & Stone Company
10 Hunter St., Albany, NY 10023

Name: _Hal Jenkins_____ Phone # _721-9093_

Item ordered _____ Cost: _____

Item ordered: _____ Cost: _____

Total Cost: _____

Computation: Performing computations of multiplication and division using whole numbers and decimal fractions; Performing basic measurement tasks including the use of conversion tables

DETERMINING SURFACE AREA

Surface area is the amount of surface an object contains. To find how much area an object has, you need to measure two dimensions, the *length* and the *width*.
Area = length × width

Surface area is expressed in *square* units. Area = 10 ft. × 5 ft. = 50 **square feet**

GUIDED PRACTICE

You are a floor installer. The tile floor pictured below is made of square tiles, 1 ft. long × 1 ft. wide.

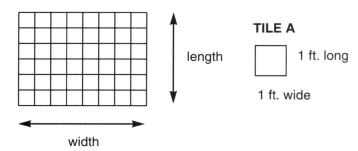

If you used Tile A:

1. a. width = _____ tiles (count the tiles)   b. The width of the floor = _____ feet

2. a. length = _____ tiles (count the tiles)   b. The length of the floor = _____ feet

You're correct if you wrote that the width is *8 feet* (8 tiles × 1 ft.) and the length is *6 feet* (6 tiles × 1 ft.).

3. Calculate the *surface area*. (length × width = area)
   _____ × _____ = _____ square feet

4. How many tiles do you need to tile this floor?_____
   (*Hint:* Take the **area of the floor ÷ area of the tile** to find the answer.
   48 sq. ft. ÷ 1 foot per tile = _____ tiles)

Practice calculating the surface area. l (length) × w (width) = A (Area)

5. l (5 ft.) × w (7 ft.) = A _____

6. l (4.5 cm) × w (6.5 cm) = A _____

7. l (12 yd.) × w (15 yd.) = A _____

You're correct if you answered: 3. *8 × 6 = 48*; 4. *48*; 5. *35 sq. ft.*; 6. *29.25 sq. cm*; 7. *180 sq. yd.*

Look at the drawing below and answer the questions that follow.

Ceiling Area

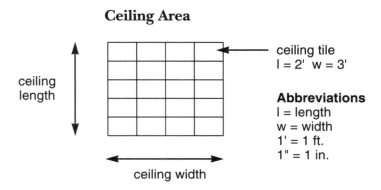

ceiling length

ceiling tile
l = 2' w = 3'

Abbreviations
l = length
w = width
1' = 1 ft.
1" = 1 in.

ceiling width

Tiles require six 3" tile stays (fasteners).

1. Find the surface area for *each tile*.
   a. What is the length? _____
   b. What is the width? _____
   c. What is the surface area? _____ × _____ = _____

                                       length   width   area

2. How many tiles will it take to retile the ceiling?
   a. What is the length? (count the tiles)_____ tiles
   b. What is the width? (count the tiles)_____ tiles
   c. What is the surface area? _____ × _____ = _____
                                       length   width   tiles

3. What is the surface area of the ceiling?
   _____ × _____ = _____
   sq. ft. per tile   total tiles   sq. ft. of ceiling

4. Circle the correct size tile stay (fastener) you need to buy.

   a.

   b.

   c.

. . . .
Computation: Solving measurement problems in U.S. Standard units using linear dimensions and area

USING CONVERSION TABLES

On most jobs, you would use the **English (U.S. customary) system** of measurement. Sometimes, though, you might use the **metric system**. In this lesson so far, you have practiced converting measurement units within the English system (feet to inches).

Some employers use both the English system and the metric system, so converting from metric to English and English to metric is a good job skill to learn.

GUIDED PRACTICE

You are a salesclerk in a fabric store. A woman says to you, "I bought this designer-style dress pattern while I was in Europe. The pattern calls for 6 meters of material. How many yards do I need to buy?"

Metric System Conversions

1 millimeter (mm) = .03937 in.

1 centimeter (cm) = .3937 in.

1 meter (m) = 3.2808 ft.
           1.0936 yd.

1 kilometer (km) = 1093.6 yd.
           .6217 mi.

To convert 6 m to yd., multiply 6 m × 1.0936 yd. = _____ yd.
You're correct if you found *6.56 yards*, which is a little over $6\frac{1}{2}$ yards.

Practice converting from metric to English using the chart above. (Round your answers to the nearest .01.)

1. 8 m = _____ yd.   8 m × 1.0936 yd. = _____ yd.

2. 26 km = _____ mi.   26 km × .6217 = _____ mi.

3. 53 cm = _____ in.   53 cm × .39379 = _____ in.

4. 79 mm = _____ in.   79 mm × .03937 = _____ in.

You're correct if you wrote: 1. *8.75*; 2. *16.16*; 3. *20.87*; 4. *3.11*.

Square Measure

English System	Metric System
1 square inch =	⌈ 645.16 square millimeters
	⌊ 6.4516 square centimeters
	⌈ 929.03 square centimeters
1 square foot =	│ 9.2903 square decimeters
	⌊ 0.092903 square meter
1 square yard =	0.83613 square meter
1 square mile =	2.5900 square kilometers
0.0015500 square inch =	1 square millimeter
0.15500 square inch =	1 square centimeter
15.500 square inches ⌉	
0.10764 square foot ⌋ =	1 square decimeter
1.1960 square yards =	1 square meter
0.38608 square mile =	1 square kilometer

Use the conversion chart above to calculate the following conversions. (Round answers to the nearest whole number.)

Example:

50 sq. in. × 6.4516 sq. cm = 323 sq. cm

1. 50 sq. cm = _____ sq. in.   50 × .155 = _____ sq. in.

2. 43 sq. m = _____ sq. yd.   43 × 1.196 = _____ sq. yd.

3. 109 sq. ft. = _____ sq. m   109 × .092903 = _____ sq. m

4. 7 sq. km = _____ sq. mi.   7 × .38608 = _____ sq. mi.

5. 84 sq. dm = _____ sq. ft.   84 × .10764 = _____ sq. ft.

6. 2,000 sq. mi. = _____ sq. km   2,000 × 2.59 = _____ sq. km

UNDERSTAND LINEAR MEASUREMENTS

You work for Franco's Home Repair. Mrs. Thomas needs to repanel her porch wall. She would like an estimate on how much this will cost. You have to figure out how many panels she will need before you can give her an estimate of cost. The dimensions of her porch wall are 8 ft. by 10 ft.

Look at the sketch shown below. Then answer the questions that follow.

1. What is the width of the porch wall? _____

2. What is the height? _____

3. What is the surface area? (width × height)_____

4. If each panel is 2 ft. × 4 ft., what is the area of each panel?

   _____

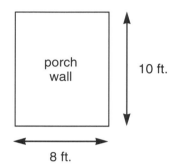

5. How many panels will it take to repanel the wall?

   _____ ÷ _____ = _____
   (surface area)   (area of each panel)   (number of panels)

WORKWISE

Find the surface area of a floor in your home. Room: _____ Area: _____

Go to the carpet store and tell them you are pricing carpets. Pick out three carpets, and tell the sales clerk how much carpet you would need. Observe how the clerk calculates the cost. Write down the cost of your first choice, and calculate how much it would cost by multiplying the surface area × cost = total cost.

   _____ × _____ = _____
   surface area   cost   total cost

· · · · · · · · · · · ·
Computation: Performing basic measurement tasks determining length, width, height, weight, including the use of conversion tables

WEIGHTS AND MEASURES

Measuring weight is a part of our daily lives. We weigh ourselves on a bathroom scale, for example, and we weigh apples in the grocery store. Postal workers weigh packages to decide how much postage is needed to ship them. Deli clerks fill an order for 2 pounds of lunch meat at the grocery store. Truck drivers pull into a truck weighing station to have a truck load weighed. Many jobs use weight measurement.

SKILL PREVIEW

You are a chef's assistant in a fine restaurant. Chef Genevieve, a French chef, uses the metric system. She asks you to measure some ingredients.

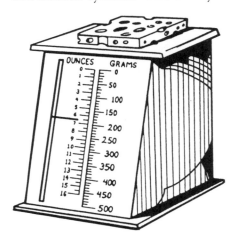

Note:
- On the **ounces scale** (left), the distance from one line to the next is $\frac{1}{2}$ ounce.

- On the **grams scale** (right), the distance from one line to the next is 10 grams.

Example: The weight of the piece of Swiss cheese can be read on both scales:

Weight: approximately $6\frac{1}{2}$ oz. or 185 grams (between 180 and 190)

Use the scale above to complete the following list. Convert the grams to ounces. Estimate your answers to the nearest $\frac{1}{2}$ ounce.

1. grated Parmesan cheese   200 grams = _____

2. chopped green onion   300 grams = _____

3. water chestnuts   150 grams = _____

4. black walnuts   350 grams = _____

5. bananas   50 grams = _____

UNDERSTANDING WEIGHT MEASUREMENTS

If you pick up a 10-pound bag of potatoes in one hand, and one apple in another, you can tell which one is heavier.

The **weight** of the apple could be written in several units of equal value:

$$\text{apple} = .5 \text{ lb.} = \tfrac{1}{2} \text{ lb.} = 8 \text{ oz.} = .22 \text{ kg} = 226.80 \text{ g}$$

Weight measures how heavy something is. You can weigh anything:

- solid objects (cheese)
- liquids (oil)
- dry goods (oats)

There are all sizes and shapes of computerized and manual scales that use both the English and metric systems to measure weight.

Weight
- 1 short ton = 2,000 pounds = .907 metric ton
- 1 long ton = 2,240 pounds = 1.016 metric tons
- 1 pound = 16 ounces = .453 kilograms
- 1 ounce = 28.350 grams

Capacity

  liquid measure
- 1 gallon = 4 quarts = 3.785 liters
- 1 quart = 2 pints = .946 liters
- 1 pint = 16 fluid ounces = 473 milliliters

  dry measure
- 1 bushel = 4 pecks = 35.239 liters

GUIDED PRACTICE

Use the chart above to figure out the weight measurements of each item. Use a calculator if you wish. (Round numbers to the nearest hundredth.)

Example: 4 pints = __64__ fluid ounces = __1,892__ milliliters

1. 6 quarts = _____ pints = _____ liters

2. 5 short tons = _____ pounds = _____ metric tons

3. 8 ounces = _____ grams

4. 11 bushels = _____ pecks = _____ liters

You are correct if you wrote: 1. *12, 5.70*; 2. *10,000, 4.54*; 3. *226.80*; 4. *44, 387.60.*

Choose the correct weight unit for each item to be measured. Write the word(s) on the line. *You may choose more than one.*

ton(s)	ounce(s)	pound(s)	gallon(s)	gram(s)
bushel(s)	gram(s)	liter(s)	kilogram(s)	quart(s)

1. _____ of milk

2. _____ of wheat or grain

3. _____ of deli meat

4. _____ of apples

5. _____ of concrete blocks

6. _____ of tomatoes

7. _____ of cola

8. _____ of oil

9. _____ of human weight

10. _____ of sour cream

WORKWISE

Go to the grocery store. Choose five products you buy often. List the measurement units used for each product.

Item	Measurement Units
1. _____	_____
2. _____	_____
3. _____	_____
4. _____	_____
5. _____	_____

Reading: Recognizing task-related words with technical meanings
Problem Solving: Categorizing

READING GRADUATED MEASUREMENTS

Like a ruler, a **scale** has lines or marks called **increments** that represent a specific number. Scales measure large weight, like a truckload of cement blocks. They also measure smaller weight, such as fresh fruit in a market. Whenever you measure any weight:

- Identify what measurement units are being used.

English	1 ton = 2,000 pounds
(U.S. Customary)	1 pound = 16 ounces
	1 ounce = 437.5 grains
Metric	1 metric ton = 1,000 kilograms
	1 kilogram = 1,000 grams
	1 gram = 1,000 milligrams

- Check if the scale is at "0" before you start to measure.

In this computerized age, an electronic scale can measure the weight of an object before you have time to think much about it, with the touch of a few buttons. But, when computers fail, you have to use a manual scale.

GUIDED PRACTICE

You are a produce clerk. An elderly woman approaches you and asks, "Would you mind weighing a few produce items for me? My eyes aren't too good anymore, but I'd like to know about how much these will cost."

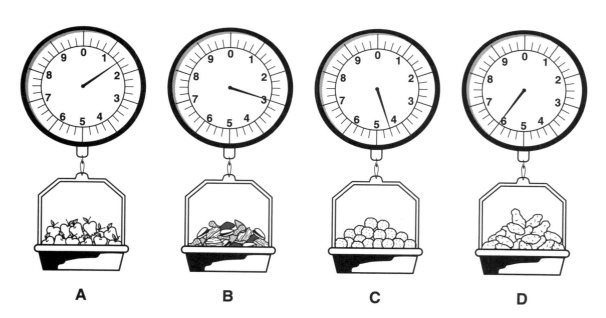

A	**B**	**C**	**D**

Look at the scale. If there are 16 ounces in each pound, how many ounces does each *increment* represent? _____ (*4 ounces* is correct.)

Use the scales shown on page 110 to find the weight measurement of the following items. Round to the nearest $\frac{1}{2}$ pound.

Example: A = __$1\frac{1}{2}$ lb.__ of apples
B = _____ of mixed party nuts
C = _____ of nectarines
D = _____ of potatoes

You are correct if you wrote: B = *3 lb.*; C = *$4\frac{1}{2}$ lb.*; D = *6 lb.*

APPLIED PRACTICE 2: READING GRADUATED MEASUREMENTS

You are the administrative assistant for Cameron Kimball, Vice President of Operations. Each time Mr. Kimball sends a package to anyone, you:

- weigh the package on a 20-pound beam scale
- **log** (write down) the weight
- determine the rate or cost of mailing the package
- log the **rate** (cost) in a daily log book
- total the log at the end of the day

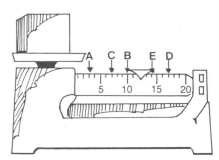

The weight for each package is noted on the scale above. Read the weight of each package and complete only the weight section on the log below.

SHIPPING LOG		
Weight	Rate	Daily Total
Package A _____	_____	_____
Package B _____	_____	_____
Package C _____	_____	_____
Package D _____	_____	_____
Package E _____	_____	_____

. . . .
Computation: Reading and interpreting basic measurement and numerical readings on measurement instruments, including identifying fractions in progressive sizes

USING APPROPRIATE MEASURING DEVICES

Scales come in all shapes and sizes. There are **mechanical** and **electronic scales**.

MECHANICAL SCALES

spring basket scale   **beam scale**   **balance scale**

 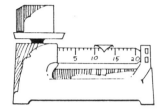 

fruits
vegetables
small unpackaged goods

parcels/packages
small grocery items

laboratory specimens
rock samples
medicine ingredients

ELECTRONIC SCALES

truck scale   **floor scale**   **electronic scale**

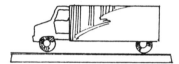  

truckload of bricks
rail car load
grain truck load

copper coil pallet
case of packaged nails
case of bottles

people
large boxes

GUIDED PRACTICE

Choose the type of scale that would be used to weigh the items listed below.

     a. spring basket scale   b. balance scale

Example: ___*a*___ one pound of potatoes

_____ 1. $\frac{1}{2}$ lb. of cheese   _____ 4. 2 apples

_____ 2. large stones   _____ 5. head of lettuce

_____ 3. capsules   _____ 6. pills

You're correct if you answered: 1. *a*; 2. *b*; 3. *b*; 4. *a*; 5. *a*; 6. *b*.

Fill in the blanks with the correct type of scale you would use to weigh each item. Refer back to page 112 if you need to.

kitchen spring scale	laboratory balance scale
floor scale	truck scale
beam scale	large electronic scale
small electronic scale	spring basket scale

1. A _____ might be used to measure the weight of unpackaged onions.

2. A _____ might be used to measure the load in a landfill dump truck.

3. A _____ might be used in a small office to measure postage on a package.

4. A _____ might be used to measure a rock specimen from a nuclear waste site.

5. A _____ might be used in a doctor's office to measure a patient's weight.

6. A _____ might be used in a glass factory to weigh a case of bottles.

7. A _____ might be used in a school cafeteria to weigh butter for a recipe.

8. A _____ might be used in a hardware store to measure 10 pounds of unpackaged nails.

9. A _____ might be used to measure the weight of a pallet of copper fixtures.

10. A _____ might be used to measure the weight of six large apples.

. . . .
Reading: Recognizing task-related words with technical meanings
Problem Solving: Categorizing

WEIGHING PACKAGES AT THE WORKPLACE

However you choose to ship a package, you'll need to weigh it first. The shipping cost may depend on the weight of the package. Shipping costs are either

- **flat rates** (the same cost for all weights) or
- **zoned rates** (the cost depends on the weight of the package and how far it is being sent)

If you are shipping under a zoned rate, you'll need to refer to a rate chart. Then you'll multiply **weight of package** × **zone rate** = **cost.**

GUIDED PRACTICE

Mario is sending out five packages today to local areas by priority mail.

Write the *weight* of each package (A to E) labeled on the scale. Then find the *rate* on the chart and list it on the log below.

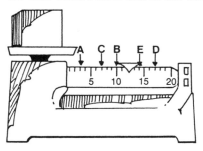

PRIORITY MAIL

Weight, up to but not exceeding— pound(s)	Local 1, 2, and 3
1	2.90
2	2.90
3	4.10
4	4.65
5	5.45
6	5.55
7	5.70
8	5.90
9	6.10
10	6.35
11	6.75
12	7.15
13	7.50
14	7.90
15	8.30
16	8.70
17	9.10

Example: To find the weight, count the number of lines to point A (3 pounds). To find the rate, look down the column to 3 and across to $4.10.

SHIPPING LOG

	Weight	Rate
Package A	3 lbs.	$4.10
Package B		
Package C		
Package D		
Package E		

You're correct if you wrote: A. *3 lbs. at $4.10*; B. *10 lbs. at $6.35*; C. *7 lbs. at $5.70*; D. *17 lbs. at $9.10*; E. *14 lbs. at $7.90.*

You work for a wholesale flower distributor. You have just received an order.

You can mail six starter plants in a box. Your company is authorized to mail third class.

Write the weight of each set of plants below the spring basket scales.

1. Queen Cerise Yarrow
   (4 starters)

   Weight = _____ oz.

2. Asiatic Lily
   (4 starters of equal weight)

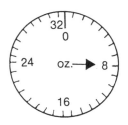

   Weight = _____ oz.

3. White Cone Flower
   (4 starters)

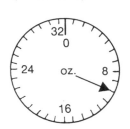

   Weight = _____ oz.

THIRD-CLASS

REGULAR AND SPECIAL BULK RATES AVAILABLE ONLY TO AUTHORIZED MAILERS—CONSULT POSTMASTER FOR DETAILS

Circulars, books, catalogs, and other printed matter; merchandise, seeds, cuttings, bulbs, roots, scions, and plants, weighing less than 16 ounces.

Single-piece rates
for piece not exceeding

1 oz.	$0.29	8 ozs.	$1.33
2 ozs.	0.52	10 ozs.	1.44
3 ozs.	0.75	12 ozs.	1.56
4 ozs.	0.98	14 ozs.	1.67
6 ozs.	1.21	Over 14 but less than 16 ozs.	1.79

Use the third-class rate chart shown above to answer the questions.

4. In the first box, you mail all four starters of Queen Cerise Yarrow, and two starters of Asiatic Lily. How much does this package weigh? _____ What is the postage rate? _____

5. In the second box, you mail the remaining two starters of Asiatic Lily and four starters of White Cone Flower. How much does this package weigh?_____ What is the rate? _____

. . . .
Computation: Reading and interpreting basic measurement and numerical readings on measurement instruments; Computing costs

CONVERTING WEIGHT UNITS

The weight units you have measured may not always be the units you need to find **prices.** For example, say you have a truckload that is measured in tons. However, your price chart measures in pounds. To find the price, you'll have to convert the weight units from tons to pounds. You can convert weight units by using a **conversion chart**.

GUIDED PRACTICE

On the job, you will probably have a conversion chart to use. If not, you can find conversions in the dictionary under *weight.*

> **English**
> 1 long ton = 2,240 pounds
> 1 short ton = 2,000 pounds
> 1 pound = 16 ounces
> 1 ounce = 437.5 grains
>
> **Metric**
> 1 metric ton = 1,000 kilograms
> 1 kilogram = 1,000 grams
> 1 gram = 1,000 milligrams

Nora needed to ship a package to California. The package weighed 3 pounds on the company scale. The price chart listed the weights in ounces. To find how many ounces Nora's package weighed, she had to multiply:

$$3 \text{ lb.} \times 16 \text{ ounces (in a pound)} = 48 \text{ ounces}$$

On the calculator   (3)(×)(1)(6)(=)(48)

Convert each of the weights by using the chart shown above.

1. 2.1 short tons = ? pounds   2.1 × ____ pounds = ____

2. 3,600 kilograms = ? metric tons   3,600 ÷ ____ kilograms = ____

3. 5.35 pounds = ? ounces   5.35 × ____ ounces = ____

4. 1,888 grams = ? kilograms   1,888 ÷ ____ kilograms = ____

You are correct if you answered: 1. *2,000, 4,200 lb.*; 2. *1,000, 3.6 metric tons*; 3. *16, 85.6 oz.*; 4. *1,000, 1.9 kg.*

You work for a grain cooperative. Local farmers come to the cooperative to buy and sell many types of grain. Your job requires you to convert weight units.

Corn, oats, and wheat are sold by the bushel (volume). As a co-op clerk, you would convert the measurement taken from a **truck scale** using the following formula:

Gross weight – Tare weight = Net weight

$$\downarrow \qquad\qquad \downarrow \qquad\qquad \downarrow$$

(weight of truck   –   (weight of   =   (weight of
with load of grain)   empty truck)   grain only)

The net weight in pounds is converted to weight in bushels. This is based on an average weight of a bushel set by the Department of Agriculture.
Based on the information above, answer the following questions.

Grain	Average Weight
corn	56 lb. per bushel
oats	32 lb. per bushel
wheat	60 lb. per bushel

1. Paul Thurston, a farmer, has come into the co-op with a truckload of corn. The gross weight is 6,985 lb. The tare weight is 4,302 lb.

   What is the net weight of the corn?
   Gross weight – tare weight = net weight
   _____ lb. – _____ lb. = _____ lb.

2. Convert the net weight of corn in pounds to short tons. You know that 2,000 lb. = 1 short ton. Divide the net weight in lb. by 2,000 lb. (1 short ton).

   Net weight _____ lb. ÷ 2,000 lb. = _____ short tons

3. Convert the net weight of corn to bushels.
   _____ lb. ÷ 56 (lb. of corn per bushel) = _____ bushels.

. . . .

Computation: Reading and interpreting basic measurement and numerical readings on measurement instruments; Computing costs

DETERMINE SHIPPING COST BY WEIGHT

You work in the office of a moving company. A customer, Mr. Franklin, calls in for a piano to be moved. It weighs 762 lb. The total trucking cost, in this case, is based upon

- flat rate for weight of the piano (which is in a crate)
- distance—100 miles free, $.15/mile after 100 miles

Use the the rate chart shown below to determine the trucking cost of Mr. Franklin's piano.

Rate Chart	
Number of lb.	**Moving Cost**
0 – 200 lb.	$ 50
201 – 500 lb.	$150
501 – 800 lb.	$250
801 – 1,000 lb.	$350

1. What is the weight of the piano? _____

2. Based on the weight of the piano, what is the flat rate for moving it? _____

3. The piano needs to be moved a distance of 345 miles. The first 100-mile cost is free. What is the moving cost for the additional mileage? _____ (no. of mi. × cost/mile = total cost)

4. Figuring the flat fee for weight and the moving cost, what is the total trucking cost that Mr. Franklin should expect to pay? _____

PRESSURE, TEMPERATURE, AND LEVELS

We use many kinds of pressure in our daily lives. We have water pressure in our showers and air pressure in our bicycle and car tires, to name just two examples.

SKILL PREVIEW

You work for Tire America. You sell and replace tires for everything from a 1963 Ford flatbed truck to an 18-wheel, double-axle Mack truck. Below you will find the air compressor gauge you use to pump air into tires. You take special precautions not to exceed the suggested pressure level.

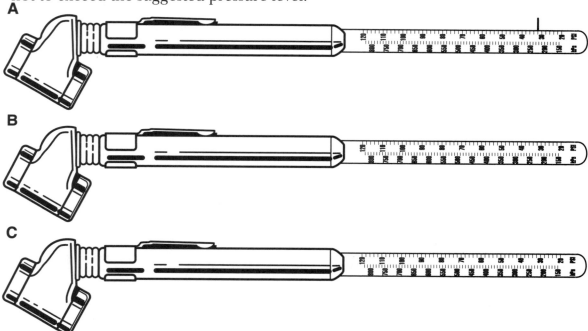

Use the information below to make a mark and label the approximate pressure level for tires B and C on the air pressure gauges above.

Example: Tire A requires 32 psi of air pressure for a domestic car tire.

1. Tire B.   40 pounds—Half-ton pickup truck tire

2. Tire C.   110 pounds—Forklift truck tire

UNDERSTANDING GAUGED MEASUREMENT

We commonly think of a **gauge** as an *instrument* that measures pressure, temperature, and levels.

PRESSURE

If you have ever pumped up your bike or car tire, you were creating a certain amount of **air pressure** in the tire.

If you have a gas heater, somewhere in your house there is a **gas gauge** that measures how much gas you use.

Pressurized gauges, like air, gas, or water gauges, not only tell you *how much pressure* but can also indicate *dangerous high or low* pressure levels.

TEMPERATURE

The most common **temperature gauge** is a **thermometer.** Many people use a thermometer to measure heat and cold in ovens or refrigerators.

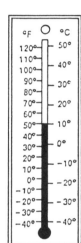

Water heater installers use a **thermometer test gauge** when they are trying to find problems with a water heating system.

LEVELS

Just like a *standard ruler* measures an inch, gauges that measure **levels** have **standards** against which you measure.

If you've been swimming, you may have seen the pool manager use a **standard level gauge** to test the pool water for chlorine levels.

Biologists and chemists run tests to check for harmful chemical levels and to determine if your drinking water is hard or soft.

Gauges for measuring the **thickness** of wire and sheet metal are used by construction workers and electricians.

Fill in the blanks to complete the statements by using one of these words.

pressure   temperature   level   thickness

1. The chlorine _____ in the pool is very high today.

2. A gas gauge measures the _____ of a propane tank.

3. When water freezes, the _____ is 32°F or 0°C.

4. The _____ of sheet metal is gauged by a standard scale.

5. When your tire is flat, there is little or no air _____ .

You're correct if you answered: 1. *level;* 2. *pressure;* 3. *temperature;* 4. *thickness;*
5. *pressure.*

APPLIED PRACTICE 1: UNDERSTANDING GAUGED MEASUREMENT

Use the pictures of gauges below to answer what might be measured by each gauge
shown. Write *a* (pressure); *b* (temperature); *c* (level); or *d* (thickness).

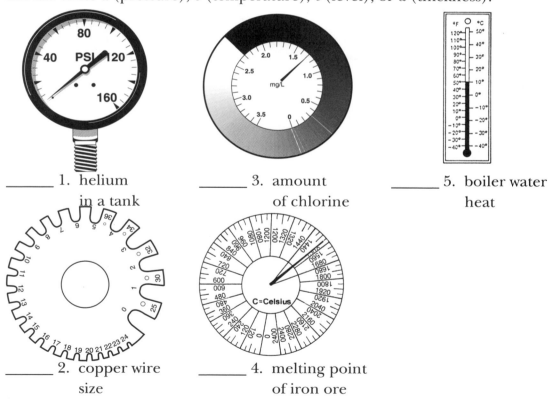

_____ 1. helium
in a tank

_____ 3. amount
of chlorine

_____ 5. boiler water
heat

_____ 2. copper wire
size

_____ 4. melting point
of iron ore

· · · · · · · · · · · ·
Computation: Reading and interpreting basic measurement and numerical readings on
measurement instruments, e.g., gauges

READING GAUGES

Gauges come in many shapes and sizes.

Air, gas, water, and electricity gauges are examples of gauges with a *face*. The face of each gauge has numbers and hands that indicate the measurement. Some gauges indicate measurement in both the English and metric systems.

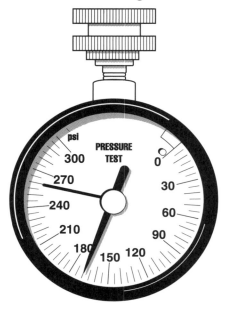

Reading a gauge is similar to measuring on a ruler or meter stick. Each **increment,** or space, represents a specific amount. The **full tank capacity**, or amount of pressure the tank can hold, is shown on the dial as the highest number.

GUIDED PRACTICE

You work for Donahue Gas Company. Customers rent helium tanks to fill balloons for large parties, weddings, or graduations. Because different size tanks have different volumes, you need to be familiar with reading several gauges. Read the following gauges.

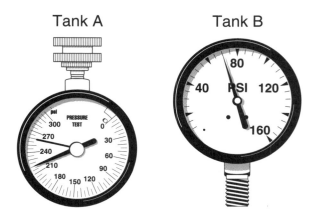

Tank A   Tank B

Answer the following questions about Tank A and Tank B on page 122.

		Tank A	Tank B
1. What is full tank capacity?		_____ psi	_____ psi
2. What does each increment represent?		_____ psi	_____ psi
3. What reading does the hand indicate?		_____ psi	_____ psi

You're correct if you answered: 1. *Tank A—300, Tank B—160*; 2. *Tank A—5, Tank B—5*; 3. *Tank A—220, Tank B—70.*

APPLIED PRACTICE 2: READING GAUGES

You are the assistant to the plant maintenance engineer at United Dairy Farmers. You are responsible for testing the water supply pressure at certain points. If the water pressure is not within a certain range, the system is not working properly and you need to report it to the engineer.

Complete the checklist in the chart below. Record the gauge reading for points A to C. Check if each pressure reading falls within the acceptable range by putting a check mark (✔) under *yes* or *no*.

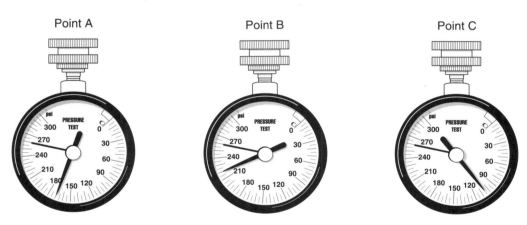

Acceptable Range 100–200 psi			
Checklist	Reading	Yes	No
Point A			
Point B			
Point C			

. . . .
Computation: Reading and interpreting basic measurement and numerical readings on measurement instruments, e.g., gauges

READING THERMOMETERS

Thermometers measure **temperature.** Most thermometers measure temperature in both Fahrenheit (°F) and Celsius (°C) readings.

You may have a **weather thermometer** outside your kitchen window so you can check how warm or cold it will be when you go outside.

Thermometers comes in all shapes and sizes. You may be most familiar with a **clinical thermometer** used in doctors' offices, medical clinics, and hospitals. As you know, clinical thermometers measure body temperature.

Water heater installers, heating and air conditioning installers, nurses, medical assistants, candy factory workers, and hotel restaurant cooks all use thermometers to measure temperature.

GUIDED PRACTICE

You work for MacLane's, a water heater installation and repair company. When you go on a repair call, some systems already have a standard thermometer in place. But you should always carry a temperature test gauge with you. It will help you find out where the problem is in a customer's system.

Your first call is at the Lemmel home. Answer the questions about the cold and hot water temperature readings shown below.

Cold water temperature   Hot water temperature

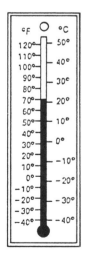 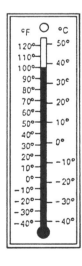

1. The cold water temperature reading is _____ F, _____ C.

2. The hot water temperature reading is _____ F, _____ C.

You're correct if you wrote: 1. *70°F, 20°C*; 2. *100°F, 40°C.*

Your next call is at the Folk Arts and Crafts Store. Answer the questions about the readings on the test gauges shown below.

Cold water temperature   Hot water temperature

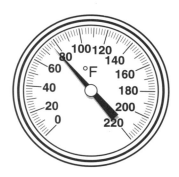   

3. The cold water temperature reading is _____ F.

4. The hot water temperature reading is _____ F.

You're correct if you answered: 3. *76°F;* 4. *140°F.*

APPLIED PRACTICE 3: READING THERMOMETERS

You work for Buster's Bakery. You've been having problems with certain breads baking properly. After five bad batches, the store owner asks you to do a test, to see if the oven is going bad.

Read the temperature on each thermometer below. Then record the temperatures in the space provided.

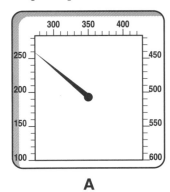   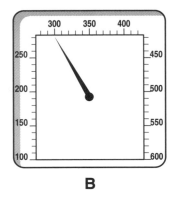   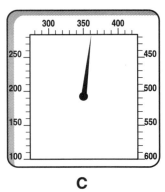

A   B   C

Time	Thermostat Setting	Actual Temperature
1. 7:45 A.M.	A. 325°F	A.
2. 9:45 A.M.	B. 375°F	B.
3. 2:15 P.M.	C. 450°F	C.

. . . .

Computation: Reading and interpreting basic measurement and numerical readings on measurement instruments, e.g., gauges

FINDING PRESSURE AND LEVELS

Have you ever taken a helium balloon outside in cold weather? What happened? Did it lose its ability to float? A helium balloon deflating in cold temperature is a great example of how pressure is affected by temperature. The hotter the temperature, the higher the pressure. The colder the temperature, the lower the pressure.

Pressure gauges measure capacity in both the English (U.S. customary) and metric measurement units.

> **English system** pounds per square inch (psi)
>
> **Metric system** kiloPascal (kPa)

Air, water, steam, and gases (like helium), are measured in **psi** (pounds per square inch) or **kPa** (kiloPascal).

Have you ever gotten into a pool and smelled the chlorine because it was so strong? Too much chlorine in a pool is an example of a potentially harmful level.

GUIDED PRACTICE

You work for Technical Testing Labs. The Lab performs chemical tests on various companies' waste. Anju, a chemist, uses **nitrous oxide** to test for levels of iron in the waste. You are responsible for setting up certain tests, making sure there is enough nitrous oxide in the tank for that particular test. When the tank is below 500 psi, you call for a replacement.

Study the following pressure gauges. *(Hint:* the kPa **readings** (numbers) are on the outside of the gauges. The psi **readings** (numbers) are on the inside of the gauges.

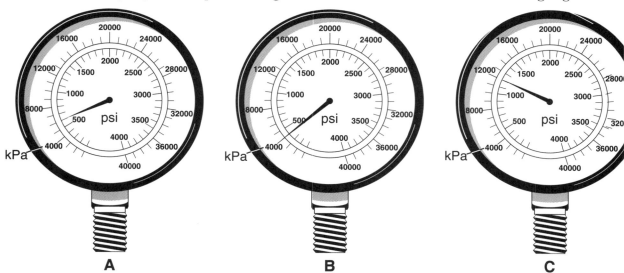

A   B   C

Use the gauges on page 126 to find the tank capacity pressures for B and C, and record the readings below.

Example: A. _**600**_ psi

1. B. _____ kPa   2. C. _____ psi

3. At which tank pressure reading (A to C) would you have called for a replacement? _____ psi

You answered correctly if you wrote: 1. B *4,000*; 2. C *1,200*; 3. *below 500 psi.*

APPLIED PRACTICE 4: FINDING PRESSURES AND LEVELS

In addition to reading the **tank capacity**, you are responsible for checking the **regulator pressure gauge**. The regulator allows only a certain amount of pressure to be released during the test. You can release the excess pressure through a release valve. If the pressure is more than the range, an explosion can occur. If the pressure is less than the range, the test will not be valid.

1. Find the pressures on the regulator pressure gauges below and record the readings in the space provided.

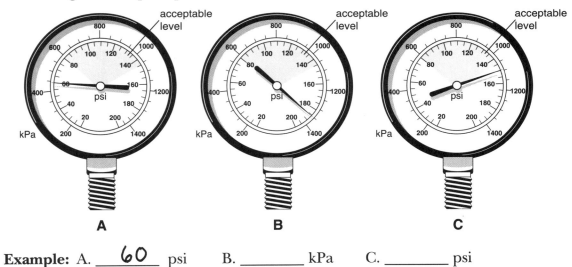

Example: A. _____**60**_____ psi   B. _____ kPa   C. _____ psi

2. Circle the reading that is an acceptable level of pressure for this test:
   A   B   C

. . . .
Computation: Reading and interpreting basic measurement and numerical readings on measurement instruments, e.g. gauges

READING FRACTIONS AND DECIMALS ON A GAUGE

There are many different kinds of gauges. In this lesson, we have presented several different kinds of gauges and thermometers.

Although the gauges in this lesson have dealt with whole numbers, some gauges deal with smaller measurements of fractions and decimals.

GUIDED PRACTICE

Study the two gauges and then record the readings for points A to F on the lines next to each gauge.

To read a whole number gauge:

Locate the smallest number on the gauge and familiarize yourself with the direction the gauge is to be read (top to bottom, bottom to top, clockwise ↺, or counter-clockwise ↻.)

Follow the same method to read fractions and decimals on a gauge:

Locate the smallest number.
How does it read?
(Top to bottom,
bottom to top,
clockwise ↺,
or counter-clockwise ↻.)

You're correct if you answered:
A. *50;* B. *85;* C. *135;* D. *0.3;* E. *3.0;* F. *1.8.*

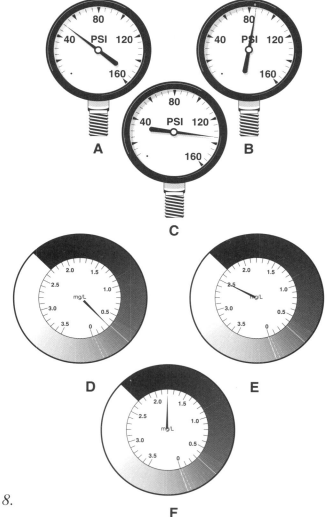

Find the chlorine level on each test gauge below.

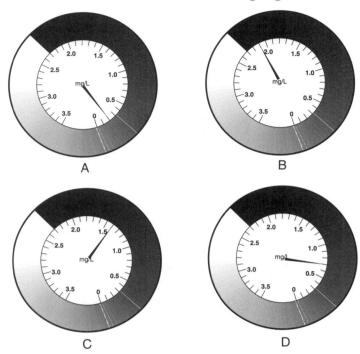

Write the correct chlorine level (mg/l) for each gauge.

Gauge   1. A _____   2. B _____   3. C _____   4. D _____

WORKWISE

Go to your local hardware and building supply store. Locate a standard wire gauge and write down the measurement of three pieces of wire. Ask for help if you need to. Fill in the measurements below.

1. _____

2. _____

3. _____

. . . .
Computation: Reading and interpreting basic measurement and numerical readings on measurement instruments, e.g., gauges

INTERPRET A PRESSURE GAUGE

You are a chemistry lab technician. You monitor the highly explosive acetylene during tests, using a specially designed gauge.

If the needle falls below 10 psi, the test is invalid, and you are to tell the chemist. If the needle approaches 15 psi, you must also tell the chemist. If the needle crosses over into the danger red zone, you turn the pressure valve off.

Use the following gauges to answer the questions.

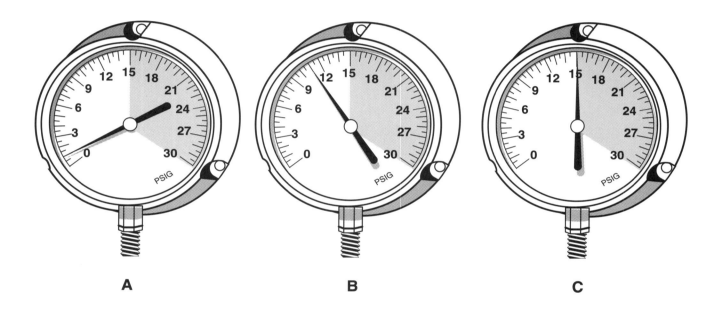

A   B   C

1. What is the pressure measurement of gauge A? _____

2. What is the pressure measurement of gauge B? _____

3. What is the pressure measurement of gauge C? _____

4. What is the dangerous pressure zone range (in psi)? _____

TIME AND MONEY

In the fast pace of doing business, sometimes we don't always make the best decisions. Understanding how money and time are related can help you make better business decisions both as a customer and as an employee.

SKILL PREVIEW

You work for Rentco, a rent-to-own store. Customers have the option to rent a product and then buy it by paying a certain amount of money each month. A customer, Ms. Harbison, comes into your store and asks you some questions about renting a television she saw advertised in the newspaper. She shows you the following advertisement:

RENT TO OWN

A 20" Fisher Color Television.

You pay *only* $12.99* a week rental fee for *only* 18 months!

*Does not include a $7.50 one-time processing fee paid with the first weekly payment. Fees subject to 6% sales tax.

Based on the advertisement, answer the following questions.

1. How much will the weekly fee including tax be? $13.76 or $17.98?

2. How much will the first payment be? $21.71 or $14.29?

3. What will my monthly payment be? $63.49 or $55.04?

4. What is the total cost of this TV? $753.34 or $990.72?

UNDERSTANDING UNITS OF TIME

When we think of **time measurement**, we may most commonly think of

> 1 minute (min.) = 60 seconds (sec.)
> 1 hour (hr.) = 60 minutes
> 1 day = 24 hours
> 1 week (wk.) = 7 days
> 1 year (yr.) = 365 days

But bank tellers, loan processors, accountants, payroll clerks, salesclerks, and purchasing agents work with more specific **units of time.** Time must be factored into figuring out discounts, costs, payment plans, and interest payments.

Some specific terms that describe units of time are

- daily, weekly, monthly, yearly (annually)
- bi-weekly (every two weeks)
- quarterly (every three months)
- semi-annually (every six months)
- bi-annually (has two meanings: twice a year, or every two years)

GUIDED PRACTICE

As a loan processor, you may have to complete calculations for several **time periods** before a customer decides which loan is the best option. The time periods you use in most of your calculations are expressed in **months.**

Make a quick reference list of time period equivalents by filling in the blanks below.

Example: ___3 months___ = quarterly (every three months, four times per year)

1. _____ months = semi-annually

2. _____ months = yearly or annually

3. _____ months = $1\frac{1}{2}$ years

4. _____ months = 2 years

5. _____ months = 3 years

You're correct if you answered: 1. *6*; 2. *12*; 3. *18*; 4. *24*; 5. *36*.

You are a loan processing clerk. Your bank has recently changed its computer system throughout the company. Now you must complete calculations using **years** or **partial years.**

Create a quick reference equivalent list by filling in the blanks.

Example: _____1/365_____ year = daily

1. _____ year = bi-weekly

2. _____ year = semi-annually

3. _____ year = 12 months

4. _____ years = 18 months

5. _____ years = 24 months

6. _____ years = 36 months

WORKWISE

Go to the bank where you do business or choose another bank in your area to visit. Pick up brochures that answer questions about these three types of accounts: CD (certificate of deposit), money market, and tax-free annuity:

1. How long does my money get locked in—90 days, 6 months, 2 years, or longer?

2. What's the penalty for withdrawing my money before the maturity date?

3. What's the rate of interest for this account?

Type of Account	How Long Money Gets Locked In	Penalty for Withdrawal	Interest Rate
CD (certificate of deposit)			
Money market			
Tax-free annuity			

. . . .
Computation: Calculating with units of time

CONVERTING UNITS OF TIME

You have seen job announcements or ads that read:

- $16,000 a year starting salary
- $6.50 an hour starting wages
- 3.25% interest earned quarterly
- 48-month used-car loan for 8%

You can **convert**, or change, **units of time** (like hours, days, and years) to check the accuracy of your paycheck, to estimate salaries for a budget, or to calculate quarterly interest earned on a savings account.

To convert units of time, we often use **standards** like

24 hours	=	1 day
7 days	=	1 week
4 weeks	=	1 month

But, some units may not be standard. For example, when you calculate payroll, eight hours may equal one working day.

The important thing to remember is: define the units before you begin your work. (8 hours = 1 work day)

You are an accounting clerk for Altex Electronics Company. The owner of the company has just hired a new electrician crew chief for a new crew.

He says, "Gus McElroy's salary is $1,650 per month. Can you get him on the payroll today?"

You say, "Sure." You have a computerized accounting system that calculates **base rate per hour only**. So you need to calculate Gus's monthly rate to an hourly rate. The average working month = 21 days, and Gus works 8 hours per day.

Convert Gus's salary to an hourly rate. Round your answer to the nearest cent.

$$\underline{\qquad\qquad\qquad} \div \underline{\qquad\qquad}/\text{month} \div \underline{\qquad\qquad}/\text{day} = \underline{\qquad\qquad}$$
(monthly salary)   (days)   (hours)

You're correct if you wrote: *$9.82 per hour ($1,650 ÷ 21 ÷ 8).*

Gus McElroy comes to you, the payroll clerk, and hands you the following list of names and base pay rates of his newly hired crew.

List	
Michael Harwood	$55/day
Manuel Gomez	$240/wk.
Jake Jones	$50/day
Roberta Brown	$1,000/mo.

Conversions

8 hours = 1 work day

5 days = 1 work week

21 days = 1 work month

Use the list and conversions above to convert the base pay rates to hourly rates. You may use a calculator if you wish. Round each rate to the nearest cent.

1. What is Michael Harwood's hourly rate?

   _____ ÷ _____ = _____
   (day)   (hr./day)   (hourly rate)

2. What is Manuel Gomez's hourly rate?

   _____ ÷ _____ = _____
   (wk.)   (hr./wk.)   (hourly rate)

3. What is Jake James's hourly rate?

   _____ ÷ _____ = _____
   (day)   (hr./day)   (hourly rate)

4. What is Roberta Brown's hourly rate?

   _____ ÷ _____ ÷ _____ = _____
   (month)   (days/mo.)   (hr./day)   (hourly rate)

. . . .

Computation: Interpreting ratio and proportion, e.g., preparing mixtures figuring pay rate; Performing Computations of addition, subtraction, multiplication, and division, including multiple operations using whole numbers

VALIDATING PAY RATES AND AMOUNTS

It is important to look at the amounts on your paycheck to see if they are correct. Be sure to check your pay stub to see if each of these amounts are correct:

- **pay** (base rate)—earnings per hour, day, or month
- **total hours** or **days** worked
- **gross pay** (wages)—total earnings before deductions
- **deductions** (amounts taken out of your pay for taxes, a retirement plan, or a medical/dental benefit plan)
- **net pay** (earnings you take home after deductions)

GUIDED PRACTICE

You are a payroll clerk. Your department has recently become completely computerized. Last month, several mistakes were made in hours worked, gross pay, and deductions. You want to make sure the computerized checks are correct. You begin with Margo Johnson's check.

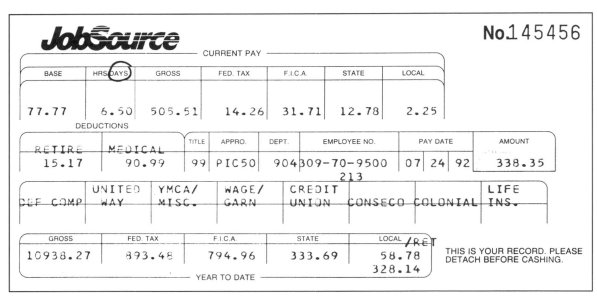

Calculate the answers for the following questions.

1. What is Margo's pay, or base rate? $ _____ /day

2. How many days did Margo work this pay period? _____ days

3. What is Margo's gross pay earned in this pay period? You may use a calculator if you wish. Round to the nearest cent.

   base/pay rate × hours/days worked = gross pay

   _____   _____   _____

Refer to Margo's check on page 136. Calculate her **net,** or take-home, pay. Margo's deductions are: federal tax, F.I.C.A. (social security), state tax, local tax, retirement, and medical benefits. (**gross pay – deductions = net pay**)

4. Margo's net pay is $ _____ for this pay period.

5. The F.I.C.A. (social security) deduction should be 7.65% of Margo's gross pay. Is the F.I.C.A. deduction shown on page 136 correct? _____

You answered correctly if you wrote: 1. *$77.77/day*; 2. *6.5 days*; 3. *77.77 × 6.50 = $505.51 (gross pay)*; 4. *$338.35*; 5. *no.*

APPLIED PRACTICE 3: VALIDATING PAY RATES AND AMOUNTS

You next look at Frank Giannini's check stub. His base rate is $9.24/hour. Use 8 hours/day to convert his hourly rate to a daily rate.

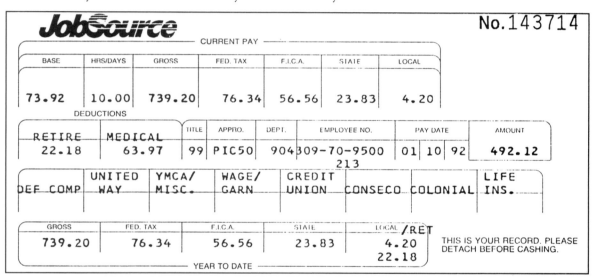

BASE	HRS/DAYS	GROSS	FED. TAX	F.I.C.A.	STATE	LOCAL
73.92	10.00	739.20	76.34	56.56	23.83	4.20

DEDUCTIONS

RETIRE	MEDICAL	TITLE	APPRO.	DEPT.	EMPLOYEE NO.	PAY DATE			AMOUNT
22.18	63.97	99	PIC50	904	309-70-9500 213	01	10	92	492.12

DEF COMP	UNITED WAY	YMCA/ MISC.	WAGE/ GARN	CREDIT UNION	CONSECO	COLONIAL	LIFE INS.

GROSS	FED. TAX	F.I.C.A.	STATE	LOCAL /RET
739.20	76.34	56.56	23.83	4.20 22.18

THIS IS YOUR RECORD. PLEASE DETACH BEFORE CASHING.

YEAR TO DATE

Calculate the answers to the following questions. Round your answers to the nearest cent.

1. Is Frank's check calculated at the correct base rate? _____

2. How many days did Frank work this pay period? _____

3. Calculate Frank's gross pay earned this pay period. $_____.

4. Is the gross pay amount correct on Frank's check? _____

5. Calculate Frank's net pay. Frank's net pay should be _____.

6. Is the net pay amount correct on Frank's check? _____

. . . .

Computation: Performing computations of addition, subtraction, multiplication, and division, including multiple operations using whole numbers

UNDERSTANDING INTEREST RATES

Interest can be defined as

- the amount of money it costs for you to borrow money
  (You pay interest on a car loan.)
- the amount of money you earn when a bank uses your money
  (You earn interest on a savings account.)

To find interest, use the formula:

$$\textbf{Principal (P)} \times \textbf{Rate (R)} \times \textbf{Time (T)} = \textbf{Interest (I)}$$

Principal is the amount of money you save or borrow.

Rate is the **percent** at which you borrow or save money.

Time is the number of days, months, or years you save or borrow money.

GUIDED PRACTICE

You are a bank teller. Daniel Dresden, a customer, comes in and asks you the annual interest on his $1,500 savings. Your bank's savings rate is 4% for one year. What is his interest?

$$\underline{\hspace{2cm}} \times \underline{\hspace{2cm}} \times \underline{\hspace{2cm}} = \underline{\hspace{2cm}}$$
(principal)　(rate/%)　(time)　(interest)

You're correct if you found Mr. Dresden's interest amount to be *$60 ($1,500 × 4% × 1).*

You can also convert the percent rate to a decimal in the formula and get the same amount. (*4%* can also be expressed as *.04* in decimal form.)

$$\underline{\hspace{2cm}} \times \underline{\hspace{2cm}} \times \underline{\hspace{2cm}} = \underline{\hspace{2cm}}$$
(principal)　(rate/in decimal form)　(time)　(interest)

You're correct if you found Mr. Dresden's interest to be *$60 ($1,500 × .04 × 1).*

What would the interest be if the principal was $1,200 at 4% for one year? ____.

You're correct if you answered: *$48.*

Some savings accounts have interest compounded quarterly. For example, using Juan Lopez's $2,500 savings and annual interest rate of 3.5%, during the **first quarter**, Mr. Lopez would have earned $21.88. Here's how:

$2,500 (balance) × .035 (rate) × .25 (quarter of year) = *$21.88*

APPLIED PRACTICE 4: CALCULATING INTEREST RATES

You are a bank teller at Providence Bank & Trust Company. Juan Lopez comes in with his family. They have just moved to Providence from out of state. The Lopez family would like to open a savings account for each family member. You explain that the bank's savings account interest rate is 3.5% for one year.

Mr. Lopez hands you a list with the savings amounts for each family member. Calculate the *annual interest* (3.5%) for each family member's savings and write it on the list below. Round each amount to the nearest cent.

Name	Amount	Annual Interest
1. Juan	$2,500	_____
2. Emily (his wife)	$2,800	_____
3. Gregory (18-year-old son)	$1,500	_____
4. Mary (15-year-old daughter)	$ 700	_____
5. Joy (7-year-old daughter)	$ 200	_____

6. Calculate the quarterly interest rate on Emily's savings amount at 3.5%.

   $_____ × .035 × .25 = $_____

7. Calculate the quarterly interest rate on Gregory's savings amount at 3.5%.

   $_____ × _____ × _____ = _____

. . . .
Computation: Performing computations of addition, subtraction, multiplication, and division, including multiple operations, using decimal fractions, percentages

CALCULATE REAL COSTS

You are a loan processor. Calculate the following interest rates and real costs based on the information given below. You may use a calculator if you wish.

Mr. and Mrs. Walker want to pay off a few bills. They apply for a $2,500 loan with 13.25% interest for 2 years.

Use the formulas:

Interest (I) = Principal (P) × Rate (R) × Time (T)

Real cost = Loan amount + Interest

1. Calculate the simple interest on the $2,500 loan the Walkers are requesting.

   _____ × _____ × _____ = _____
   (P)   (R)   (T)   (I)

2. What is the real cost the Walkers will pay back to the bank?

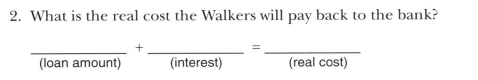

   _____ + _____ = _____
   (loan amount)   (interest)   (real cost)

3. Calculate the simple interest if the Walkers applied for a loan of $5,600 with 15% interest for 3 years.

   _____ × _____ × _____ = _____
   (P)   (R)   (T)   (I)

4. What is the real cost the Walkers will pay back to the bank?

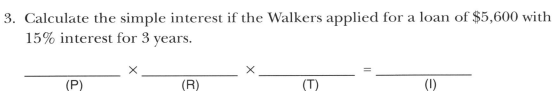

   _____ + _____ = _____
   (loan amount)   (interest)   (real cost)

ANSWER KEY

UNIT I: OFFICE SERVICES AND ADMINISTRATION

TELEPHONE MESSAGES

SKILL PREVIEW

Page 5

1. George Lee
2. John Williams
3. George Lee needs an extra 1,000 envelopes on this month's order.
4. on April 3 at 2:45 P.M.
5. (612) 555-5609

APPLIED PRACTICE 1:
LISTENING FOR KEY POINTS

Page 7

Your telephone message should contain this information:

Check with plant manager, shift chief, and quality control inspector to see if they can meet tomorrow.

Suggested times: 10:00 tomorrow morning or 10:00 Wednesday morning

Who is involved: 1. plant manager, 2. shift chief, 3. quality control inspector

APPLIED PRACTICE 2:
CLARIFYING THE MESSAGE

Page 7

Are Mr. Canty, Mr. Smith, and Ms. James free for a meeting at 10:00 tomorrow morning or at 10:00 Wednesday morning?

APPLIED PRACTICE 3:
RECORDING NUMBERS CAREFULLY

Page 8

1. (639) 882-4102, 639/882-4102, or 639-882-4102
2. (202) 636-0203, 202/636-0203, or 202-636-0203
3. (530) 796-2408, 530/796-2408, or 530-796-2408

APPLIED PRACTICE 4:
USING NEWS WRITING METHODS

Page 10

Who: Mr. Trask

What: You and your partner must sign the two contracts you requested.

Where: in your attorney's office

When: by the close of business tomorrow

Why: to meet the deadline

How: send them by messenger

APPLIED PRACTICE 5:
RECORDING TIME ACCURATELY

Page 10

1. 4:30 P.M.
2. 9:45 A.M.
3. 11:00 P.M.
4. 8:45 A.M.

APPLIED PRACTICE 6:
WRITING LEGIBLY

Page 11

Did you answer the questions? If you did, they were guesses, since the information was not written clearly. Even a check mark can be confusing if it is carelessly written.

APPLIED PRACTICE 7:
CHECKING FOR COMPLETENESS

Page 12

Possible questions you could ask:

1. What is Anne's last name?
2. What is Angela's last name?
3. How many tutors are needed?
4. Where is the youth center located?
5. When should Anne meet Angela with the tutors?
6. Was the call made at 7:45 A.M. or P.M.?

APPLIED PRACTICE 8:
SUGGESTING A SOLUTION

Page 13

Possible solutions: install a more efficient phone system; change the procedure so that editors get their calls more quickly

SKILL MASTERY
Page 14
Your form should look like this:

```
TO:  _Ray Douglas_____

Time: _10:50 A.M._____  Date: _2/2_____

Please Call:

_____Kim Wong, President of First Central Bank_

Telephone # _____(454) 232-0800_____

Message: _We need a go-ahead on your loan,___
_____and at least one hour's notice._____

_____

                              Operator:  Lynn Moon
```

REFERENCE MATERIALS
SKILL PREVIEW
Page 15
1. table of contents
2. scan
3. title
4. index
5. caption
6. skim
7. chart

APPLIED PRACTICE 1:
SELECTING REFERENCE MATERIALS
Page 16
1. *Nursing Assistant Manual*
2. *Machine Repair Manual*
3. *Zip Code Directory*
4. *Workplace Safety Manual*
5. *Computer Manual*

APPLIED PRACTICE 2:
READING A TABLE OF CONTENTS
Page 18
1. Chapters 16–19
2. Chapter 2
3. 670
4. Chapter 25
5. 109
6. Chapter 21
7. 14
8. Chapter 15
9. Chapters 25–27

APPLIED PRACTICE 3:
READING AN INDEX
Page 19
1. 592–593
2. 221–222
3. 98
4. 92
5. 146–150
6. 351–352

APPLIED PRACTICE 4:
SKIMMING
Page 20
Paragraph 1: 2; paragraph 2: 2

APPLIED PRACTICE 5:
SCANNING
Page 21
1. 350°F
2. for about $1\frac{1}{4}$ to $1\frac{1}{2}$ hours
3. every 15 minutes
4. onion

APPLIED PRACTICE 6:
SCANNING A CHART
Page 23

1. 14.40
2. snapper
3. 80
4. bluefin tuna
5. 3.36
6. sole
7. 91
8. sole
9. squid
10. swordfish
11. striped bass
12. 118

SKILL MASTERY
Page 24

1. 5
2. 20
3. 4
4. 14
5. 3

POLICY MANUALS
SKILL PREVIEW
Page 25

Your form should look like this:

```
VACATION REQUEST FORM
Employee's name: your name          Date submitted: July 10
Vacation dates/time requested:    July 24-30
Employee's signature:    your name
Department: Sporting Goods   Supervisor's name: Donna Novak
-------------------------------------------------------------
Supervisor's signature: _____
Approved:   Yes / No    Date dis/approved: _____
```

APPLIED PRACTICE 1:
UNDERSTANDING THE PURPOSE OF POLICY
Page 27

Use these answers as a guideline.

1. A policy states a course of action, a rule, or a plan.
2. Employees refer to their policy manual for hiring procedures, conditions of employment, pay plans, benefits, and expected conduct.

APPLIED PRACTICE 2:
READING A POLICY MANUAL
Page 27

1. for the control of personnel activities for JobSource
2. (3) to provide fair and equal opportunity to all qualified people

APPLIED PRACTICE 3:
READING A POLICY MANUAL'S INDEX
Page 29

1. XI, 31
2. IV, C
3. 10–11, 32
4. IV, O
5. N
6. IV, I

APPLIED PRACTICE 4:
FINDING THE MAIN IDEA OF A PARAGRAPH OR SECTION
Page 31

1. to describe disciplinary steps supervisors will take if employees show misconduct or poor performance on the job
2. Discipline must be handled the same for every employee regardless of their rank within the company.
3. an employee and his or her supervisor
4. it is placed in the employee's Personnel File; to document what has taken place and to make sure the supervisor and employer are both in agreement as to the content of their conversation.

APPLIED PRACTICE 5:
IDENTIFYING SEQUENTIAL DIRECTIONS
Page 33

Your wording should be similar to the following:

Step 1: Employee submits resignation in writing to his/her Director two weeks prior to date of resignation.

Step 2: Employee receives approval of his/her Director.

Step 3: Director forwards resignation request to the Human Resources Director.

Step 4: Employee requests final evaluations from his/her Director, Human Resources Director, and Executive Director one week prior to resignation date.

Step 5: Copies of final evaluations from Directors are forwarded to Personnel for employee records.

6. The employee shall be subject to discharge.

APPLIED PRACTICE 6:
MAKING INFERENCES FROM A TEXT
Page 35

1.	7	5.	1a
2.	1b	6.	1c
3.	4	7.	1b
4.	6 or 7	8.	5

SKILL MASTERY
Page 36

Your resignation letter should look like this:

```
                              (your home address)


Mr. Hank Napoli
Mitchell and Boone
112 Canal
Lockport, MN 43986

April 6, 1993

Mr. Napoli:

This letter is to inform you that I am resigning from Mitchell and
Boone effective April 20, 1993. I am leaving to start another job
with the law firm of Townsend, Yosha, and Cline.

I appreciate all I have learned at Mitchell and Boone during the
past three years. I look forward to a new opportunity for growth
in my career.

Sincerely,
(your name)
```

UNIT II: PURCHASING AND SELLING

CHARTS AND TABLES
SKILL PREVIEW
Page 39

1. $7.05
2. $4.60
3. $5.25
4. $3.40
5. $1.20
6. $7.80
7. $2.25
8. $4.40
9. $6.00
10. $10.00
11. $1.65
12. $6.20

APPLIED PRACTICE 1:
USING SALES TAX
Page 41

1. a. .03
   b. .035
   c. .06
   d. .08
   e. .085
   f. .10
2. a. .65
   b. $13.64
3. a. $112.35
   b. $1,610.35
4. a. $21.89
   b. $569.24

APPLIED PRACTICE 2:
USING A FIXED-RATE TAX TABLE
Page 42

1. $6.75 + .48 + .06 = $7.29
2. $10.25 + .80 + .02 = $11.07
3. $9.00 + .72 = $9.72
4. $7.50 + .56 + .04 = $8.10
5. $17.00 + .80 + .56 = $18.36

APPLIED PRACTICE 3:
USING A MULTI-RATE TAX TABLE
Pages 42–43
Part A
Your invoice should look like this:

P&R Printing

Miller Mall
244 Main Street
Littletown, AL 36123
(205) 555-1212
FAX (205) 555-0230

Date _____   Number of Copies **47**

SERVICE	QUANTITY	UNIT PRICE	TOTAL
FAX			
Phone Time			
8½ x 11	47	.08	$3.76
8½ x 14			
Other			
Collate			
Supplies			
SUB-TOTAL			
TAX			.30
TOTAL			$4.06

WORLD'S LARGEST PRINTING CHAIN

Part B

1. Quantity 40, Price $3.20, Tax .26, Total $3.46
2. Quantity 46, Price $3.68, Tax .29, Total $3.97
3. Quantity 42, Price $3.36, Tax .27, Total $3.63; or Quantity 43, Price $3.44, Tax .27, Total $3.71
4. Quantity 50, Price $4.00, Tax .32, Total $4.32
5. Quantity 49, Price $3.92, Tax .32, Total $4.24

APPLIED PRACTICE 4:
USING A SALE DISCOUNT TABLE
Page 45

1. $13.00 − (.75 + 2.50) = 3.25 = $9.75
2. $26.00 − (3.00 + 10.00) = 13.00 = $13.00
3. $23.00 − (.75 + 5.00) = 5.75 = $17.25
4. $18.00 − (4.00 + 5.00) = 9.00 = $9.00

APPLIED PRACTICE 5:
USING A VARIABLE-RATE DISCOUNT TABLE
Page 46

1. a. $1,000
   b. $200
2. a. $30
   b. $50
3. a. $20
   b. $60
4. a. $10.00
   b. $6.00

APPLIED PRACTICE 6:
COMPUTING DISCOUNTS
Page 47

1. $8.49, $11.20, $16.98
2. $4.33, $5.71, $8.65
3. $5.38, $7.10, $10.75
4. $11.24, $14.83, $22.48

SKILL MASTERY
Page 48

1. a. yes
2. a. no
   b. .76, $10.26

PRODUCT INFORMATION FOR SELLING

SKILL PREVIEW
Page 49

1. Sensitive Eyes
2. no
3. no
4. yes

APPLIED PRACTICE 1:
READING LABELS AND INSTRUCTIONS
Page 51

1. yes, water
2. around the plant roots
3. Use one tablespoon per gallon of water for every plant. Apply every two weeks.
4. yes
5. You should break up large lumps with a dull tool. Mixed with water, the hard lumps will dissolve easily.
6. every two weeks
7. No, it is not recommended.

APPLIED PRACTICE 2:
IDENTIFYING TARGET AUDIENCE
Page 53

2. acid indigestion
3. sour stomach
4. upset stomach

APPLIED PRACTICE 3:
COMPARING FACTUAL DETAILS
Page 54

1. flat, semi-gloss, $7.99 (flat) or $10.99 (semi-gloss)
2. cracking, peeling, $16.99
3. no-scuff, $14.99

APPLIED PRACTICE 4:
IDENTIFYING A PRODUCT'S KEY FEATURES
Page 55

1. Robitussin
2. 3.5%
3. expectorant
4. no
5. no
6. 2–4 teaspoonfuls every four hours, not to exceed 12 teaspoonfuls in a 24-hour period
7. 1–2 teaspoonfuls every four hours, not to exceed 6 teaspoonfuls in a 24-hour period

APPLIED PRACTICE 5:
RELATING PRODUCT FEATURES AND BENEFITS
Page 57

What the customer wants in a tire:

1. to keep control of his car on tight winding curves
2. to have the kind of tread to brake suddenly

Features

3. center stabilizing rib

4. computer designed tread

Customer Benefits

directional stability and steering control for optimum traction and braking

SKILL MASTERY
Page 58
Possible questions you might ask include:
1. Are you allergic to aspirin?
2. Do you have asthma?
3. Do you have chicken pox or flu symptoms?

4. Do you have stomach problems, such as heartburn, upset stomach, or stomach pains, that persist?
5. Do you have ulcers or bleeding problems?
6. Are you pregnant or nursing a baby?
7. Are you taking a prescription drug for thinning the blood or for arthritis?

The product label will contain the product features, benefits, and dosage for children and adults. Use the label as a guide.

PRODUCT INFORMATION FOR PURCHASING
SKILL PREVIEW
Page 59
The purchase order should be completed like this:

<table>
<tr><th colspan="6">PURCHASE ORDER   3785</th></tr>
<tr><td colspan="6">TO   Decker's
ADDRESS   19 W. 9th St.
SHIP TO   Ace Super Supply
ADDRESS   841 Rhodes, Rm. 402, Anaheim, CA 90001</td></tr>
<tr><td>REQ. NO.</td><td colspan="2">FOR</td><td colspan="3">DATE</td></tr>
<tr><td colspan="2">DATE REQUIRED
9-20</td><td colspan="2">HOW SHIP
U.P.S.</td><td colspan="2">TERMS
C.O.D.</td></tr>
<tr><th>QUANTITY</th><th colspan="3">PLEASE SUPPLY ITEMS LISTED BELOW</th><th>PRICE</th><th>UNIT</th></tr>
<tr><td>1   40</td><td colspan="3">Red Sanford Sharpie Markers</td><td>24 | 00</td><td>.60</td></tr>
<tr><td>2   30</td><td colspan="3">Green Sanford Sharpie Markers</td><td>18 | 00</td><td>.60</td></tr>
<tr><td>3</td><td colspan="3"></td><td></td><td></td></tr>
<tr><td>4</td><td colspan="3"></td><td></td><td></td></tr>
<tr><td>5</td><td colspan="3"></td><td></td><td></td></tr>
<tr><td>6</td><td colspan="3"></td><td></td><td></td></tr>
<tr><td>7</td><td colspan="3"></td><td></td><td></td></tr>
<tr><td>8</td><td colspan="3"></td><td></td><td></td></tr>
<tr><td>9</td><td colspan="3"></td><td></td><td></td></tr>
<tr><td>10</td><td colspan="3"></td><td></td><td></td></tr>
<tr><td>11</td><td colspan="3"></td><td></td><td></td></tr>
<tr><td>12</td><td colspan="3"></td><td></td><td></td></tr>
<tr><td colspan="2">IMPORTANT
OUR ORDER NUMBER MUST APPEAR ON ALL INVOICES-PACKAGES, ETC.
PLEASE NOTIFY US IMMEDIATELY IF YOU ARE UNABLE TO SHIP COMPLETE ORDER BY DATE SPECIFIED.</td><td colspan="4">PLEASE SEND   2   COPIES OF YOUR INVOICE

(your name) PURCHASING AGENT</td></tr>
<tr><td colspan="2">REDIFORM.</td><td colspan="4">ORIGINAL</td></tr>
</table>

APPLIED PRACTICE 1:
IDENTIFYING WHERE TO FIND APPROPRIATE ADS
Page 61

1. a. the local library, b. in your workplace
2. a. newspapers, b. company brochures,
    c. catalogs, d. trade magazines
3. product, service

APPLIED PRACTICE 2:
IDENTIFYING HOW TO FIND APPROPRIATE ADS
Page 61

1. f   4. a
2. b, g   5. d
3. c   6. e

APPLIED PRACTICE 3:
COMPARING AD INFORMATION ON A GIVEN PRODUCT
Page 63

Step 1: Your product features lists should look like this:

SL570	SD670
1. 75,000-word Spell-Right dictionary	1. 7,000-word editable memory
2. WordFind	2. 16-character display
3. Full-line correction memory	3. battery backup
4. word and line eraser	4. full-line memory correction
5. auto return	5. 75,000-word Spell-Right dictionary
6. center	6. Word-Right/AutoSpell
7. underscore	7. correcting cassette
8. bold print	8. 15 lbs.
9. triple pitch	9. $169.97
10. auto page insert	
11. 14 lbs.	
12. $139.97	

Step 2:
1. Smith Corona Electronic typewriter
2. SL570
3. SL570CM

APPLIED PRACTICE 4:
FILLING OUT A PURCHASE ORDER
Page 65
Your purchase order should look like this:

PURCHASE ORDER 3752

TO: Decker's
ADDRESS: 19 W 9ᵀᴴ St Anderson IN 46015
SHIP TO: MRT Marketing Co.
ADDRESS: One Mills Rd., Bedford, WA 70770

REQ. NO. 349	FOR Mailing Dept.	DATE 4-3
DATE REQUIRED 4-10	HOW SHIP UPS	TERMS C.O.D.

QUANTITY	PLEASE SUPPLY ITEMS LISTED BELOW	PRICE	UNIT
1	3 boxes	6"x9" clasp envelopes	14 97	4.99
2	3 boxes	9"x12" clasp envelopes	19 47	6.49
3	2 boxes	4⅛"x9½" white		
4		commercial envelopes	12 78	6.39

IMPORTANT
OUR ORDER NUMBER MUST APPEAR ON ALL INVOICES-PACKAGES, ETC.
PLEASE NOTIFY US IMMEDIATELY IF YOU ARE UNABLE TO SHIP COMPLETE ORDER BY DATE SPECIFIED.
PLEASE SEND 4 COPIES OF YOUR INVOICE
your name PURCHASING AGENT
REDIFORM   ORIGINAL

PURCHASE ORDER 3754

TO: Decker's
ADDRESS: 19 W 9ᵀᴴ St Anderson IN 46015
SHIP TO: 1ˢᵀ National Bank
ADDRESS: 1313 Madison St., Toledo, OH 48806

REQ. NO. 9099	FOR Loan Dept.	DATE Mar. 4
DATE REQUIRED Mar. 5	HOW SHIP Fed Ex overnight	TERMS C.O.D.

QUANTITY	PLEASE SUPPLY ITEMS LISTED BELOW	PRICE	UNIT
1	50	green 3"x3" Post-it Notes	37 50	.75
2	100	cream 4"x 6" Post-it Notes	159 00	1.59

IMPORTANT
OUR ORDER NUMBER MUST APPEAR ON ALL INVOICES-PACKAGES, ETC.
PLEASE NOTIFY US IMMEDIATELY IF YOU ARE UNABLE TO SHIP COMPLETE ORDER BY DATE SPECIFIED.
PLEASE SEND 3 COPIES OF YOUR INVOICE
your name PURCHASING AGENT
REDIFORM   ORIGINAL

APPLIED PRACTICE 5:
COMPARING COSTS AGAINST A BUDGET
Page 67
1. 5, 25
2. 8, 80
3. 320, 32,000
4. 6, 6
5. 8, 40
6. 6, 60

UNIT III: SHIPPING AND RECEIVING

MILEAGE CHARTS AND TRANSPORTATION SCHEDULES

SKILL PREVIEW
Page 71

1. e
2. d
3. a
4. b
5. c
6. f

APPLIED PRACTICE 1:
USING A MILEAGE DISTANCE CHART
Page 73

1. 183
2. 49
3. 143
4. 113
5. 44
6. 436
7. 135
8. 255

APPLIED PRACTICE 2:
READING A TRANSPORTATION SCHEDULE
Page 74

1. Signal Mtn. Rd.
2. 6:00 P.M.
3. yes

APPLIED PRACTICE 3:
CALCULATING MILEAGE
Page 75

Day 3: 46.2 miles
Day 4: 36.5 miles
Day 5: 62 miles
Week's Total Mileage: 363.5 miles

APPLIED PRACTICE 4:
FIGURING MILEAGE
Page 76

Step 4: Mileage = 271 miles
Step 5: Miles per gallon = 38.7
Step 6: 464.4 miles per tank

APPLIED PRACTICE 5:
CALCULATING TIME AND RATE OF SPEED
Page 77

1. 3 hours
2. 1 hour
3. 4 hours
4. 55 mph
5. 55 mph
6. 65 mph

APPLIED PRACTICE 6:
COMPLETING A DELIVERY SCHEDULE
Page 79

2. 8:22 A.M.
3. 16 minutes + 8:22 A.M. = 8:38 A.M.

4. 33 minutes + 8:38 A.M. = 9:11 A.M.
5. 20 minutes + 9:11 A.M. = 9:31 A.M.
6. 27 minutes + 9:31 A.M. = 9:58 A.M.

SKILL MASTERY
Page 80

1. 1:50 P.M.
2. Palisades & Signal Mtn. Blvd.
3. Market
4. Weekday
5. 5 minutes
6. 5:20 P.M.
7. 3:55 P.M.
8. 40 minutes

SHIPPING AND RECEIVING DOCUMENTS

SKILL PREVIEW
Page 81

Your receiving portion of the freight bill should look like this:

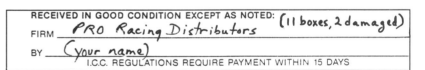

APPLIED PRACTICE 1:
LOCATING INFORMATION
Page 83

1. weight of the package or shipment
2. dimensions
3. declared value
4. destination
5. who is paying for shipping—shipper or consignor

APPLIED PRACTICE 2:
COMPARING PARCEL DELIVERY SERVICES
Page 85

1. Emery & Purolator
2. TWA
3. Emery & Purolator

Your bill of lading should look like this:

Uniform Domestic Straight Bill of Lading, adopted by Carriers in Official, Southern, Western and Illinois Classification Territories, March 15, 1922, as amended August 1, 1930 and June 15, 1941

UNIFORM STRAIGHT BILL OF LADING
ORIGINAL—NOT NEGOTIABLE.

Shipper's No. *9051*

Company

Agent's No. ....

RECEIVED, subject to the classifications and tariffs in effect on the date of the issue of this Bill of Lading.

At *10 A.M., April 9* 19*93* From *The Worth Corporation*

the property described below, in apparent good order, except as noted (contents and condition of contents of packages unknown), marked, consigned, and destined as indicated below, which said company (the word company being understood throughout this contract as meaning any person or corporation in possession of the property under the contract) agrees to carry to its usual place of delivery at said destination, if on its own road or its own water line, otherwise to deliver to another carrier on the route to said destination. It is mutually agreed, as to each carrier of all or any of said property over all or any portion of said route to destination, and as to each party at any time interested in all or any of said property, that every service to be performed hereunder shall be subject to all the conditions not prohibited by law, whether printed or written, herein contained, including the conditions on back hereof, which are hereby agreed to by the shipper and accepted for himself and his assigns.

(Mail or street address of consignee—For purposes of notification only)

Consigned to *Pro Racing Distributors*
Destination *1779 Winding Way, Daytona* State of *Florida* County of *Orange*
Route *Pick up at south entrance of shipping bay*
Delivering Carrier *Carter Express, 6015 Pendleton Ave., Anderson, IN 46013*

NO. PACKAGES	DESCRIPTION OF ARTICLES, SPECIAL MARKS AND EXCEPTIONS	* WEIGHT (Subject to Correction)	CLASS or RATE	CHECK COLUMN	
12 Boxes	*Gloves #HT8*	*562 lbs.*	*FC 220*		Subject to Section 7 of conditions, if this shipment is to be delivered to the consignee without recourse on the consignor, the consignor shall sign the following statement:
					The carrier shall not make delivery of this shipment without payment of freight and all other lawful charges.
					Signature of Consignor.
					If charges are to be prepaid, write or stamp here, "To be Prepaid."
					Received $ _____

* If the shipment moves between two ports by a carrier by water, the law requires that the bill of lading shall state whether it is "carrier's or shipper's weight."
Note.—Where the rate is dependent on value, shippers are required to state specifically in writing the agreed or declared value of the property.
The agreed or declared value of the property is hereby specifically stated by the shipper to be not exceeding $.................... per....................

Charges Advanced:

....Shipper, Per .... AGENT.................................... PER.................. ①

Permanent postoffice address of shipper..

The Fibre Boxes used for this shipment conform to the specifications set forth in the box maker's certificate thereon and all other requirements of Rule 41 of the Consolidated Freight Classification.

APPLIED PRACTICE 4: PROCESSING DOCUMENTS OF RECEIPT

Page 89

Your completed receiving record should look like this:

Receipt No. 79061		(today's date) 19(year)
RECEIVED FROM Worth Corp.		
By (your name)		
REQUISITION NO.		
In good order the following:		

QUANTITY	NO.	DESCRIPTION OF PACKAGES
10	#H39	Helmet Slips
20.	#FR14	Material

TOPS FORM 3014
LITHO IN U.S.A.
ORIGINAL

Sign here (your name)

APPLIED PRACTICE 5: USING POSTAL RATE TABLES

Page 91

1. $2.90
2. $7.65
3. $8.30
4. $5.45
5. zone 4
6. $7.00
7. $4.10

SKILL MASTERY

Page 92

Your completed receiving record should look like this:

Receipt No. 50878		(today's date) 19(year)
RECEIVED FROM Angus Metals		
By (your name)		
REQUISITION NO. 4594		
In good order the following:		

QUANTITY	NO.	DESCRIPTION OF PACKAGES
100	#8	Skids Copper Coil
		3 Damaged Skids

TOPS FORM 3014
LITHO IN U.S.A.
ORIGINAL

Sign here (your name)

UNIT IV: PRODUCTION OF GOODS AND SERVICES

MEASURING SIZE AND SPACE

SKILL PREVIEW
Page 95
1. measuring tape
2. 25 meters
3. 25 yards
4. olympic pool

APPLIED PRACTICE 1:
UNDERSTANDING UNITS OF MEASUREMENT
Page 97
1. mm
2. mi.
3. m, meter stick
4. in., ruler

APPLIED PRACTICE 2:
CHOOSING UNITS OF MEASUREMENT
Page 97
1. mm, cm, in.
2. in., ft., m
3. ft., m
4. mm, cm, in.
5. m, ft., yd.

APPLIED PRACTICE 3:
FINDING AND ESTIMATING MEASUREMENTS
Page 99
1. $\frac{7}{8}$"
2. $2\frac{1}{2}$"
3. a. 4", b. $3\frac{3}{4}$"
4. a. $2\frac{1}{2}$", b. 3"
5. a. $\frac{7}{8}$", b. 1"

APPLIED PRACTICE 4:
CONVERTING UNITS OF MEASUREMENT
Page 101
Step 1:
1. 2.5 long tons, $100 \times 2.5 = $250
2. 4 short hundredweight, $4 \times $26 = $104
Step 2:
Your order form should look like this:

Grant's Block, Brick & Stone Company
10 Hunter St., Albany, NY 10023

Name: _Hal Jenkins_   Phone # _721-9093_
Item ordered: _50 long cwt. cinder blocks_ Cost: _$250_
Item ordered: _4 short cwt. limestone_ Cost: _$104_
                                  Total Cost: _$354_

APPLIED PRACTICE 5:
DETERMINING SURFACE AREA
Page 103
1. a. 2' (2 feet)
   b. 3' (3 feet)
   c. 2' × 3' = 6 sq. ft.
2. a. 5 tiles
   b. 4 tiles
   c. 5 × 4 = 20 tiles
3. 6 sq ft. per tile × 20 tiles = 120 sq. ft. of ceiling
4. b (3-inch tile stay)

APPLIED PRACTICE 6:
USING CONVERSION TABLES
Page 105
1. 7.75 sq. in., rounded to 8 sq. in.
2. 51.43 sq. yd., rounded to 51 sq. yd.
3. 10.13 sq. in., rounded to 10 sq. in.
4. 2.7 sq. mi., rounded to 3 sq. mi.
5. 9.04 sq. ft., rounded to 9 sq. ft.
6. 5,180 sq. km

SKILL MASTERY
Page 106
1. 8 ft.
2. 10 ft.
3. 80 sq. ft.
4. 8 sq. ft
5. 80 ÷ 8 = 10 panels

WEIGHTS AND MEASURES
SKILL PREVIEW
Page 107
1. 7 ounces
2. $10\frac{1}{2}$ ounces
3. $5\frac{1}{2}$ ounces
4. $12\frac{1}{2}$ ounces
5. 2 ounces

APPLIED PRACTICE 1:
UNDERSTANDING WEIGHT MEASUREMENT
Page 109
1. gallon, quart
2. bushel
3. ounces, pounds
4. pound, grams, bushel
5. ton
6. quart, bushel, pound
7. liter, ounces
8. gallon, quart
9. pounds, kilograms
10. ounce

APPLIED PRACTICE 2:
READING GRADUATED MEASUREMENTS
Page 111
1. 3 lb.
2. 10 lb.
3. 7 lb.
4. 17 lb.
5. 14 lb.

APPLIED PRACTICE 3:
USING APPROPRIATE MEASURING DEVICES
Page 113
1. spring basket scale
2. truck scale
3. beam scale or small electronic scale
4. balance scale or small electronic scale
5. large electronic scale
6. floor scale
7. kitchen spring scale
8. spring basket scale
9. floor scale
10. spring basket scale

APPLIED PRACTICE 4:
WEIGHING AND MAILING PACKAGES
Page 115
1. 4 oz.
2. 8 oz.
3. 10 oz.
4. 8 oz., $1.33
5. 14 oz., $1.67

APPLIED PRACTICE 5:
CONVERTING WEIGHT UNITS
Page 117
1. 6,985 lb. – 4,302 lb. = 2,683 lb.
2. 2,683 lb. ÷ 2,000 lb. = 1.34 short tons
3. 2,683 lb. ÷ 56 = 47.91 bushels

SKILL MASTERY
Page 118
1. 762 lb.
2. $250
3. $36.75
4. $286.75

SKILL PREVIEW
Page 119
Your air gauges should look like this:

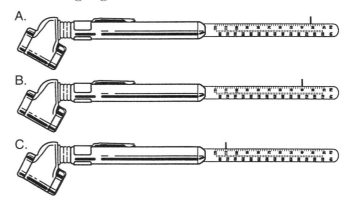

APPLIED PRACTICE 1:
UNDERSTANDING GAUGED MEASUREMENT
Page 121
1. a. pressure
2. d. thickness
3. c. level
4. b. temperature
5. b. temperature

APPLIED PRACTICE 2:
READING GAUGES
Page 123
Your chart should look like this:

Acceptable Range 100-200 psi			
Checklist	Reading	Yes	No
Point A	170	✔	
Point B	220		✔
Point C	105	✔	

APPLIED PRACTICE 3:
READING THERMOMETERS
Page 125
1. A. 260°F
2. B. 300°F
3. C. 360°F

APPLIED PRACTICE 4:
FINDING PRESSURES AND LEVELS
Page 127
1. B. 1,350 kPa
   C. 150 psi
2. none

APPLIED PRACTICE 5:
READING DECIMAL GAUGES
Page 129
1. A 0.2
2. B 2.1
3. C 1.4
4. D 0.7

SKILL MASTERY
Page 130
1. 1 psi
2. 10 psi
3. 15 psi
4. 15-30 psi

SKILL PREVIEW
Page 131
1. $13.76
2. $21.71
3. $55.04
4. $990.72

APPLIED PRACTICE 1:
UNDERSTANDING UNITS OF TIME
Page 133
1. 26/365
2. $\frac{1}{2}$
3. 1
4. $1\frac{1}{2}$
5. 2
6. 3

APPLIED PRACTICE 2:
CONVERTING UNITS OF TIME
Page 135
1. $55/day ÷ 8 hr./day = $6.88/hr.
2. $240/wk. ÷ 40 hr./wk. = $6.00/hr.
3. $50/day ÷ 8 hr./day = $6.25/hr.
4. $1,000/mo. ÷ 21 days/mo. ÷ 8 hr./day = $5.95/hr.

APPLIED PRACTICE 3:
VALIDATING PAY RATES AND AMOUNTS
Page 137
1. yes
2. 10 days
3. $739.20
4. yes
5. $492.12
6. yes

APPLIED PRACTICE 4:
CALCULATING INTEREST RATES
Page 139
1. $87.50
2. $98
3. $52.50
4. $24.50
5. $7
6. $2,800, $24.50
7. $1,500 × .035 × .25 = $13.13

SKILL MASTERY
Page 140
1. $2,500 × 13.25% × 2 = $662.50
2. $2,500 + $662.50 = $3,162.50
3. $5,600 × 15% × 3 = $2,520
4. $5,600 + $2,520 = $8,120

GLOSSARY

air freight: shipments sent by airplane

appropriate: especially suitable or fitting

area code: three digits at the beginning of a telephone number that tell the area or region where the call is being made

base rate pay: total earning, or wages, before deductions

benefits: something an employer provides employees in addition to pay, such as health insurance or paid vacation

biannually: twice a year; every two years

bill of lading: a packing slip that comes with a shipment that includes the declared value and the class of the shipment

biweekly: every two weeks

CD (certificate of deposit): a type of savings account that earns a higher rate of interest but requires a minimum deposit, which must be left in the account for a fixed period of time or a penalty must be paid for early withdrawal

COD (cash on delivery): a method of payment that requires a person to pay for a shipment when it arrives

calculate: find by performing mathematical operations; estimate

capacity: the ability to hold or contain

consignee: receiver

conversion: a change from one unit to another (pounds to grams)

cost per unit: amount charged for each item

declared value: the cost of replacement of the contents of a package

deductions: amounts taken out of a person's pay for such things as taxes, a retirement plan, or a medical/dental benefit program

delivery schedule: a plan that tells the amount of time needed to get to and from a destination point

denominator: bottom number of a fraction

disciplinary action: step taken when an employee has committed an act of gross misconduct

discount: to take off a certain percent from the original item price

documentation: paperwork showing proof that an order has been placed

documents: official papers, forms, or records that show proof that something occurred

English (U.S. Customary) System: measures in units such as inches, feet, yards, or miles

esprit de corps: enthusiastic devotion of members to a group and strong regard for the honor of the group

essential: important

estimate: a rough or approximate calculation; probable answer

F.I.C.A. (Federal Insurance Contributions Act): refers to the amount deducted from a person's paycheck as part of a government insurance program, which is paid back to the person upon retirement or because of a disability; also known as Social Security

felony: theft

fixed-rate tax tables: a chart that shows percent amounts that do not change and are added to the amount of sale

full tank capacity: amount of pressure a tank can hold

glossary: a definition section at the back of a book

gross pay: total earnings, or wages, before deductions

gross weight: overall weight of a load, including weight of container

heading: title

hindrance: something that gets in the way or holds back

increments: units being measured, e.g., lines on a ruler or scale

index: an alphabetical list of topics at the back of the book

indiscriminately: randomly

indolence: laziness

inefficiency: state of not being able to do something well; incompetence

insubordination: not obeying authority

interest: the profit in money that is earned on invested capital; the amount paid to borrow money

interest rate: the percentage of a loan or credit balance a person must pay back to a bank or credit card company

invoice: a bill given to a business when it makes a purchase

key points: important parts of a message

kpa: kilo Pascal; a metric measurement unit on a gauge

linear measurement: one dimension; for example, length or width

log: write down

malfeasance: wrongful conduct

metric system: measures in units such as millimeters, centimeters, meters, and kilometers

mileage distance chart: a boxed set of numbers that shows how far it is from one place to another in miles

misconduct: improper or unlawful behavior

money market account: a type of savings account that requires a minimum deposit that must be kept in for a fixed period of time, but the interest rate may vary daily, and there is a penalty for early withdrawal

motor freight: shipments sent by truck

multi-rate tax table: a chart that shows percent amounts added to the sale amount, depending on the quantity ordered

net pay: amount of money a person is paid after deductions have been taken out

net weight: weight of a container and its contents

numerator: top number of a fraction

odometer: an instrument that measures distance traveled by a vehicle

outline: a brief summary often in numbered divisions

pallet: a portable platform for handling, storing, or moving materials and packages (often used in warehouses, factories, or trucks)

parcel services: methods of delivering goods

pay period: the amount of time covered by one paycheck

pay stub: part of paycheck that employee keeps for his or her records; also called check stub

payroll: a list of persons entitled to receive pay with the amounts due to each

performance evaluation: a written or oral judgment about an employee's ability to do a job

point-of-sale cash register: a machine that reduces or discounts item prices as soon as they are entered

policy: a rule, plan, or course of action

policy manual: employment handbook

postage rate: amount charged for sending a package, depending on the weight and the zone, or area, to which the package is shipped

postal rate table: chart that shows the cost of shipping based on weight and zone

pressurized gauge: instrument used to measure the amount of air, gas, or water needed and to indicate dangerous high or low pressure levels

principal: the amount of money a person saves or borrows

probationary period: a period of trial for finding out or testing a person's fitness, as for a job

procedure: manner or method in which a business or an action is carried on

product benefits: parts of a product that make it attractive to a buyer

product features: parts or details contained in a product, often printed on the label

product specifications: details such as weight, color, or size

psi: pounds per square inch

purchase order: a form that someone fills out to buy equipment or supplies

purchasing agent: one who buys equipment or supplies for a workplace

quarterly: every three months

rate: the percent at which a person borrows or saves money

real cost: the loan amount plus interest

receiver: the person who takes a telephone message

receiving record: a form filled out when a shipment arrives that includes the number of packages received, the number that should have been delivered, and the condition of the shipment

reference materials: sources in which you look for information, such as books, guides, manuals, files, or computer printouts

referral: the act of guiding someone to a person or place for treatment, help, advice, or information

regulator pressure gauge: an instrument that allows only a certain amount of pressure to be released

reprimand: a severe or formal criticism

Roman numeral: a numeral in a system of figures based on the ancient Roman system, e.g., I–XV (1–15)

round down: to change a number that is less than half of the increment, or number, down to the nearest whole number ($3\frac{5}{16}$" to 3")

round up: to change a number that is half or more of the increment, or number, up to the nearest whole number ($2\frac{7}{8}$" to 3")

sabotage: destruction of an employer's property or the action of making it difficult to work by discontented workers

salary: a regular payment for working a certain number of hours per week or per month

scale: an instrument that measures distances or amounts

scan: read quickly to find specific information

semiannually: every six months

sender: person who calls in with a message

shipping label: document on a shipment that includes delivery instructions and declared value of the contents of a package

singular sale discount table: a chart that shows the percent taken off the original item price

skim: read quickly through a text to find out in general what it's about

supervisor: person in charge of employees or of a department

surface area: the amount of surface an area contains—including length and width

table of contents: a list of general topics, located at the front of a book, that are included in that book

tare weight: weight of an empty container

target audience: people who might be interested in a particular product

tax-free annuity: a type of pension plan that is free of taxation until distribution at age 59½, with a penalty if funds are withdrawn before that time

tenure: the length of time a person holds a position or an office

terms: how and when to make payment(s)

thermometer: an instrument for measuring temperature

time: the number of days, months, or years in which a person saves or borrows money

trade magazines: periodicals that advertise product and service information about a particular industry

uniformly: always having the same manner, form, or degree

unit count: number of items in a package, box, or container

variable-rate discount: amount deducted or taken off the item price, depending on how soon the bill is paid

vendors: companies that sell products or services

PURCHASE ORDER

_____

TO	
ADDRESS	
SHIP TO	
ADDRESS	

REQ. NO.	FOR		DATE
DATE REQUIRED	HOW SHIP		TERMS

QUANTITY	PLEASE SUPPLY ITEMS LISTED BELOW	PRICE	UNIT
1			
2			
3			
4			
5			
6			
7			
8			
9			
10			
11			
12			

IMPORTANT

OUR ORDER NUMBER MUST APPEAR ON ALL INVOICES-PACKAGES, ETC.

PLEASE NOTIFY US IMMEDIATELY IF YOU ARE UNABLE TO SHIP COMPLETE ORDER BY DATE SPECIFIED.

PLEASE SEND _____ COPIES OF YOUR INVOICE

PURCHASING AGENT

REDIFORM.

ORIGINAL

Uniform Domestic Straight Bill of Lading, adopted by Carriers in Official, Southern, Western and Illinois Classification Territories, March 15, 1922, as amended August 1, 1930 and June 15, 1941

UNIFORM STRAIGHT BILL OF LADING
ORIGINAL—NOT NEGOTIABLE.

Shipper's No.

Company

Agent's No.

RECEIVED, subject to the classifications and tariffs in effect on the date of the issue of this Bill of Lading.

At .... 19 .... From ....

the property described below, in apparent good order, except as noted (contents and condition of contents of packages unknown), marked, consigned, and destined as indicated below, which said company (the word company being understood throughout this contract as meaning any person or corporation in possession of the property under the contract) agrees to carry to its usual place of delivery at said destination, if on its own road or its own water line, otherwise to deliver to another carrier on the route to said destination. It is mutually agreed, as to each carrier of all or any of said property over all or any portion of said route to destination, and as to each party at any time interested in all or any of said property, that every service to be performed hereunder shall be subject to all the conditions not prohibited by law, whether printed or written, herein contained, including the conditions on back hereof, which are hereby agreed to by the shipper and accepted for himself and his assigns.

Consigned to ....

(Mail or street address of consignee—For purposes of notification only)

Destination .... State of .... County of ....

Route ....

Delivering Carrier .... Car Initial .... Car No. ....

NO. PACKAGES	DESCRIPTION OF ARTICLES, SPECIAL MARKS AND EXCEPTIONS	*WEIGHT (Subject to Correction)	CLASS or RATE	CHECK COLUMN

Subject to Section 7 of conditions, if this shipment is to be delivered to the consignee without recourse on the consignor, the consignor shall sign the following statement:

The carrier shall not make delivery of this shipment without payment of freight and all other lawful charges.

....
Signature of Consignor.

If charges are to be prepaid, write or stamp here, "To be Prepaid."

Received $ .... to apply in prepayment of the charges on the property described herein.

....
Agent or Cashier.

Per ....
(The signature here acknowledges only the amount prepaid.)

Charges Advanced:

* If the shipment moves between two ports by a carrier by water, the law requires that the bill of lading shall state whether it is "carrier's or shipper's weight."
Note.—Where the rate is dependent on value, shippers are required to state specifically in writing the agreed or declared value of the property.

The agreed or declared value of the property is hereby specifically stated by the shipper to be not exceeding $ .... per ....

.... Shipper, Per ....

.... AGENT ....

Permanent postoffice address of shipper ....

PER ....

①

The Fibre Boxes used for this shipment conform to the specifications set forth in the box maker's certificate thereon and all other requirements of Rule 41 of the Consolidated Freight Classification.

Carter Express, Inc.

6015 Pendleton Avenue
Anderson, IN 46013
Phone 317-642-8410
FAX 317-644-0052

(MC-158033)
(ICC CTID 200)

PRO NO.

DATE _____

SHIPPER _____ ADDRESS _____

CONSIGNEE _____ ADDRESS _____

3RD PARTY BILLING _____ ADDRESS _____

DRIVER: _____ TRUCK: _____ TRAILER: _____

TRANSFER TO OR FROM _____ AT _____ SHIPPER B-L # _____

NO. PCS.	DESCRIPTION	WEIGHT	RATE	PAYMENT TERMS Prepaid ☐ Collect ☐

DETENTION TIME — LOADING	DETENTION TIME — UNLOADING	
DATE _____ APPOINTMENT TIME _____	DATE _____ APPOINTMENT TIME _____	
TIME CUSTOMER NOTIFIED OF ARRIVAL _____	TIME CUSTOMER NOTIFIED OF ARRIVAL _____	**TOTAL DUE**
LOADING TIME _____ FINISHED _____	UNLOADING STARTED _____ FINISHED _____	

IF TRUCK ARRIVED BEFORE 8:00 A.M. WAS DOCK OPEN FOR BUSINESS   YES (   )   NO (   )

DELIVERY RECORD	RECEIVED IN GOOD CONDITION EXCEPT AS NOTED:
DRIVER'S NAME _____	FIRM _____
DATE _____ HOUR _____	BY _____
	I.C.C. REGULATIONS REQUIRE PAYMENT WITHIN 15 DAYS

WHITE — Office Use   YELLOW — File Copy   PINK — Customer Copy   GOLDENROD — Payroll

TERMS: A FINANCE CHARGE OF 1½% PER MONTH (ANNUAL RATE OF 18%) WILL BE CHARGED ON BALANCES OVER 30 DAYS.

Receipt No._____ _____19_____

RECEIVED FROM_____

By_____

_____

REQUISITION NO._____

_____

In good order the following:

QUANTITY	NO.	DESCRIPTION OF PACKAGES

TOPS FORM 3014
LITHO IN U. S. A.
ORIGINAL

Sign here _____